SHIPS & SEAMEN

END-PAPERS
Dutch flagships close inshore
by W. Van de Velde

Christopher Lloyd

in collaboration with

J. Douglas-Henry

SHIPS &

FROM THE VIKINGS T

Turkish and Maltese galleys
in action, early 16th century

SEAMEN

THE PRESENT DAY: A HISTORY IN TEXT AND PICTURES

THE WORLD PUBLISHING COMPANY

CLEVELAND AND NEW YORK

Contents

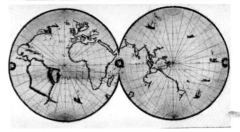

Published by The World Publishing Company, 2231 West 110th Street, Cleveland 2, Ohio
Copyright © 1961 by Christopher Lloyd. All rights reserved. Printed by Istituto Italiano d'Arti Grafiche, Bergamo, Italy. Library of Congress Catalog Card Number: 61-5991

Acknowledgements

The publishers acknowledge with thanks the following sources for the illustrations: *Accademia, Venice,* 29; *Artinano,* ' La Arquitetura ¡Naval Espagnola ' 37, 40, 61; *Asmolean Museum,* Oxford, 24; *Bibliothèque Nationale,* Paris, 27, 28, 100, 149, 300, 303, 311, 351; *Bodleian Library,* Oxford, 6, 88; *Bourges Cathedral,* 13; *Alan Bowness Esq,* 268; *Prof. C. R. Boxer,* 242; *British Museum,* London, 1-2, 14-17, 19-21, 32, 36, 38, 43-6, 48, 53, 59, 74, 81, 84-5, 92-4, 99, 101-4, 108-9, 134, 139, 162, 181, 192, 195, 203, 241, 324-5; *de Bry's* ' America ', 57; *J. Cranmer Byng Esq,* 167; *Cunard Steamship Co.,* 346, 348, 350, 382, 401; *the Dicksons, Plymouth, Mass.,* 98; *Hakluyt Society,* London, 55; *Her Majesty's Stationery Office,* 322; *Hulton Picture-Post Library,* 68; *Illustrated London News,* 292-4, 312, 315, 360-1, 369-70; *Imperial War Museum,* 296, 374-5, 379, 381, 383-5, 387-8, 391-4, 396-7; *Sir Bruce Ingram, Navy Records,* 233; *Italia Shipping Line,* 402; *Humphrey Joel Esq,* 319; *Kemp and Lloyd,* ' The Brethren of the Coast ', 153, 155; *King's College,* Cambridge, 69; *Magdalene College,* Cambridge, 71, 121. 145; *Mariners Museum, Newport News, Va.,* 286-90, 301, 308-9, 339, 344, 347. 349, 365, 371-2; *R. K. Morris Collection,* 378; *Musée de la Marine,* Paris, 39, 41, 138, 143-4, 146, 174, 186, 259, 271-2, 336, 342, 377; *National Gallery,* London, 137; *National Maritime Museum,* Greenwich, Jacket, end-papers, 7-12, 18, 23, 25-6, 30-1, 33-5, 42, 50-2, 54, 56, 58, 70, 72-3, 76-80, 82, 86-7, 89-91, 96-7, 105-7, 110-7, 122-3, 125-7, 129-33, 135, 140-2, 151-2, 154, 156-61, 163-7, 168-73, 175, 177-9, 182-5, 187-91, 194, 196-8, 200-2, 204-27, 230-2, 234-5, 239-40, 243-55, 257-8, 260-2, 273-7, 282, 297-9, 302, 310, 313-4, 316-8, 323, 337-8, 353, 355-6, 358-9, 362-4, 366-8, 373, 376, 380; *National Portrait Gallery,* London, 95, 244, 256, 326; *Nelson Studio,* Greenwich, 284; *New York Public Library,* 291; *Oslo Museum,* 3-5; *Peabody Museum of Salem,* 266, 278, 280, 290; *Plymouth City Museum,* 83; *Paul Popper Esq.,* 328; *Portuguese Information Service,* 47, 49, 60; *Royal Geographical Society,* 327; *Royal Navy,* official photo, 265; *Ryksarchiv,* the Hague, 193; *Ryksmuseum,* Amsterdam, 118-9; *Scheepvart Museum,* Amsterdam, 22, 136, 237-8; *Science Museum,* London, 75, 120, 124, 148, 176, 199, 243, 263, 267, 269-70, 281, 283, 285, 329; *Sjohistoriska Museum,* Stockholm, 128, 147, 150; *Svenska Flottens,* Historia, 180; official *United States Navy* photographs, 386, 389-90, 395, 398, 403-6; *Messrs Vickers-Armstrong,* 400; *Victory Museum,* Portsmouth, 228-9, 264; *Capt. A. J. Villiers,* 330-5

FOREWORD

In our own day, for all the comfort and security made possible by modern science, the sea is still a tender enemy, and a harsh friend. Imagine, then, the terror of navigation before ships were properly adapted to the huge forces they must encounter, when to be out of sight of land was to lose touch with certainty, and to stand too close inshore was to deliver the ship to destruction. The Greeks and Phoenicians were tentatively probing the Atlantic coasts of Europe in the fourth century BC, and the Romans ruled the Mediterranean with their cruel triremes. But the first to gain real confidence in ocean-going ships were the Vikings, whose bold voyages beyond the western horizon brought them as far as the shores of America itself. Their slight warships made a path through the oceans. Henceforward, the history of nations was in large part the history of seapower. One by one the great maritime powers arose — Venice, Portugal, Spain, the Netherlands, France, Germany, Italy, Britain and the United States. The experience and disasters of war, the countless lonely voyages of trade and exploration, gradually changed the design of ships, until, within a few short decades, the invention of the iron hull and marine steam engine transformed the navies and merchant fleets of the world.

Ships were at their most beautiful when great artists were available to portray them. The graceful lines of the ships and their rigging have been preserved in paint, pencil and scale-models, long after the originals have disappeared, and in the last century the camera has revealed the splendour and intricacy of modern ships of war and peace. It is upon such illustrations that the present book is based. Its range is international. All the nations of the western world have made their contribution to man's knowledge and conquest of the sea, and from each in turn have come great admirals, explorers and ship-designers. Each has also provided, generation after generation, the humbler seamen and deckhands who have manned the ships, and it is to them that a large part of this volume is devoted. Men have added by their pugnacity to the natural perils of sea-faring, but war and tempest have jointly created the brotherhood of the sea, for wherever there is danger, there will be found a sense of comradeship.

1

The hermit St Guthlac is rowed in a fishing boat to the island of Crowland in the Lincolnshire marshes in 699 A.D. From a twelfth century scroll

CHAPTER I
Ships of the Northern Seas

When the Roman legions weakened and the Vikings came down from their northern seas to plunder the British Isles and the continental seaboard, there were no navies to engage their dragon ships at sea; nor, when it came to fighting on the land, were there many warriors to match the fierce bands who manned these superb ships. They were masters of the sea. They held the British Isles repeatedly to ransom, and many cities of Western Europe paid them vast sums to stay away. One of their expeditions reached the walls of Paris by way of the River Seine. They took away great spoils, but in return they brought their knowledge of the sea and their skill at building ships.

We do not know precisely when these ships first came into use along the western shores of Europe, nor can we tell the distances they may have sailed, but recent research has established beyond any doubt that the Vikings discovered and named the American continent five hundred years before Columbus. Among the Viking heroes who made this voyage, Leif Ericsson is known to have landed there early in the eleventh century, and he named the country Vineland, or Markland. The deeds of such men as Leif and his crew were told abroad by the minstrels of his day, in obscure, interminable, allusive sagas so beloved of the Nordic races. Men in other lands — lands which were to profit greatly from Vineland, rediscovered at a later date — were unimpressed by the news, or quite oblivious to it. It came before its time. The urge for adventure and a lust for gold were the motives for these voyages, and there was in them no idea of trade, of conquest or of cargo. But of the quality of the Viking ships there can be no doubt. According to the story of St Guthlac, such ships were in use in the seventh century, and other versions were still being built seven hundred years later.

3 *below*
The rebuilt Gokstad ship (in the Viking museum at Oslo) dates from the tenth century. Excavated at Gokstad, Norway, in 1880, she was used as the ship-grave of a Viking chief. 23 metres long, she was clinker-built (planks overlapping) as a warship. The crew's shields were fixed to the sides to give them extra freeboard when at sea; the line of holes beneath them took the oars. She carried a single mast

2 *above*
The carved beak on the stern-post of a Viking ship was intended to propitiate the tutelary spirits of the deep. This example, probably eighth century A.D., was found in the River Scheldt

The Oseberg Ship

The skeleton of a Viking Queen lay in this funerary ship excavated at Oseberg in Norway. She dates from about 900 A.D. The lines of these Viking ships were perhaps the most beautiful ever designed. Known as snake or dragon ships, they were clinker-built and double-ended, and their tall stem and stern posts were decorated with intricately carved motifs. Like the landing craft of our own day they were of shallow draught, which enabled them to beach easily or penetrate far up rivers, and they had a low freeboard which was raised at sea by fixing a row of overlapping shields on the outside of the gunwales. Loose floor-boards were used instead of a deck, there were benches for oarsmen, and amidships a single mast carried a square sail and was supported by a rudimentary form of backstay. In the reign of King Canute (1017-35) sixty-oared ships were built, some three hundred feet long. In 1893 a reconstructed Viking ship of this type was sailed across the Atlantic Ocean for display at the Chicago exhibition.

Some years after Leif Ericsson landed on the distant shores of the hitherto undiscovered continent of America, William of Normandy invaded England. He came in long ships of the Viking build and he brought his cavalry with him. The ships of his invasion fleet carried masts supported by shrouds as well as by backstays, which enabled his ships to sail not only before the wind, as the Vikings did, but also with the wind abeam.

4 above

Stern view of the Oseberg ship, showing the transverse tiller-bar fixed to the head of the short steering oar. This oar was usually fixed to the right-hand side of the ship, which thus came to be known as the 'steering board', and later 'starboard', side

5 right

The Oseberg ship, discovered in 1904, dates from the ninth century. She was 21 metres long, and was powered by thirty oars, a wonderful example of Viking construction and decoration. Contemporary Mediterranean ships were built on a different principle inherited from the Romans, with their planks laid edge to edge on the frames

6
A miniature from an early medieval manuscript illustrating the story of Jonah and the
whale. The ship is of the Viking type, double-
ended with a single mast

HIC NAVIS ANGLI CA VENIT INTER RAM WILLELMI DU CIS

HIC EXEUNT CABALLI DEN AUIBUS

12

THE BAYEUX TAPESTRY

is thought to have been produced in England by the order of Bishop Odo of Bayeux, soon after the Norman conquest of England in 1066. These scenes, extracted from the great length of the tapestry, illustrate William the Conqueror's invasion

7

Messengers arrive on the coast of Normandy in long-ships of the traditional northern build, bringing the news that Harold has been made King of England. Duke William immediately gives orders for an invasion fleet to be built

8

Suitable timber is selected, felled and split into planks which the shipwrights trim with hatchets until the desired shape is achieved. On completion, the ships are launched at St Valéry on the Norman coast

9

As William's ships ground at Pevensey, sails are lowered and the masts struck. Armoured cavalry advance up the beach, bound for the battlefield of Hastings

10

Seal of Winchelsea, c. 1300. The ship is getting under way. Hands in the bows pass the anchor lines aft to men working a windlass. A sailor climbs aloft by way of the backstays. A figure in the sterncastle grasps the tiller, while heralds announce the ship's departure

11

Seal of Dover, c. 1305. The banner of the Baron of the Cinque Ports flies at the masthead. The castles fore and aft are more substantial structures than was usual at this period, and the 'tops' or crows-nest, above the main yard, is here shown for the first time

12

Seal of Stralsund, Sweden, c. 1329. This is a round ship, sometimes called a 'nef' or 'cog'. The tall stem or stern posts have gone; the sterncastle is now part of the hull; the recently invented rudder, hung from the stern posts, has replaced the steering oar

13

A ship of 1400, from a stained glass window at Bourges. She belonged to Jacques Coeur, a famous merchant of the period. The sails are now raised with block and tackle, and in the tops sheaves of spears and arrows are carried for defence

The Round Ship

Some time before 1400, a new trend in hull and rig design was developed to meet the requirements of merchants carrying cargoes by sea. The Viking ships were well suited for a surprise attack on a coastal town, or a swift raid up-river, but they were too narrow for purposes of trade. Already in the thirteenth century, shipbuilders in Britain and on the Continent were launching primitive versions of the round ship, as these new-type vessels came to be called. They were ships of wider beam and deeper draught, built to carry cargo below, and a great weight of gear aloft. The loose floor-boards of the Viking ships became the deck planks of the round ships, and the tall, curving stem and stern posts gave way, for wartime purposes, to fore- and stern-castles — shaky, insubstantial structures at first, but later made permanent and elaborately carved. Stouter masts were stepped to carry the bigger sail areas, and these were furnished with crow's-nests, to provide a platform for a lookout man on peaceful voyages, and in war an excellent battle station for bowmen and spearmen, who also dropped large stones upon hostile heads below. In their beginnings, these round ships were still single-masted and clinker-built, but the seals of the Cinque Ports and other busy seaports of the period show very well the changes that had already taken place. Some inventor thought of shipping a bowsprit; there were great improvements in standing

and running rigging; and the steering oar was replaced by a rudder hung on the stern post and worked by a tiller. Then, as often happens, the exigencies of war taxed the inventiveness of ship designers and gave a great impulse to the shipbuilding industry and its technique. During the Hundred Years War, in the first half of the fourteenth century, Edward III's fleet included a ship with guns mounted upon her decks. She was the *Christopher of the Tower*, and in 1330 she fought and defeated the French at Sluys.

14 *above*

A sea-battle before ships carried guns. Naval warfare in the early Middle Ages was limited to close fighting between shiploads of soldiers armed with land weapons. To fall overboard in heavy armour was fatal. From a manuscript in the British Museum

15

A naval encounter in 1416. Genoese crossbowmen are sailing before the wind to attack one of the Earl of Warwick's ships. The Earl's crest — the Bear and Ragged Staff — is seen on the pennant of the English ship. The stone-thrower aloft is pierced through the body by an arrow. From a manuscript account of the expedition during the Hundred Years War

15

16 *above*

A warlike fleet under way in the fifteenth century. Sailors, ignored by the anxious soldiery, are steering the ships and attending to the rigging. The ammunition hoists to the tops carry nothing more lethal than stones

17 *right*

A royal fleet of French ships, blazoned with heraldic shields, setting out for the coast of Barbary. The expedition includes a vessel of the galley type, shown in the foreground of the picture. From Froissart's Chronicles

Sea Battles Before Gunpowder

Although there was no Royal Navy, in the sense of a body of men and ships permanently in the service of the Crown, England was at this time a naval power to be reckoned with. In times of crisis, privately owned ships were hired by the Sovereign, who put guns and soldiers aboard and sent (or led) his ships into battle. An executive Captain directed the fighting, his soldiers worked the guns, and the standing officers, the master and crew who manned the ship in peace and war, attempted to execute such tactical manoeuvres as the Captain might require during the course of the engagement.

The technique of ship construction continually improved, and as the demand for cargo space grew with the increase of trade, larger ships were built to meet it. It became more than ever necessary that these richly laden vessels should be able to protect themselves, and in the fifteenth century a Frenchman from Brest, Descharges, thought of piercing the sides of a ship with gun ports, which made it possible to carry aboard guns of far greater calibre. These 'great ships', as they were called, achieved a displacement of some 400 tons. They stepped two or three masts and mounted ten or twelve guns below the main deck. They engaged in coastal traffic, they went to sea as pirates if their owners were so inclined, and they made regular voyages south to the Barbary Coast or north to Russia and the Baltic.

18
A late fifteenth-century seal from Maldon, Essex, showing a 'great ship' with her sides pierced for guns. On her mainsail appear the arms of the town

19 *above*
Three-masted 'nefs', with covered decks fore and aft, were being built by the mid-fifteenth century. The ribs of the ship are clearly seen, as well as the spars and a spare anchor

20 *left*
A page from the History of Quintus Curtius, executed for the Duke of de Vere of Zeeland in 1500, illustrating a great ship engaging field-pieces on shore. The projecting forecastle, well shown in this example, became a feature of early Tudor ships

17

Methods of Navigation

A knowledge of celestial bodies and their movements in the night skies smacked of witchcraft and black magic in the early Middle Ages, and most mariners of that time found their way across the sea by a method of dead reckoning, and they sailed along an ascertainable latitude. In other words, they relied upon the northward pointing needle of a compass to tell them the direction in which their ship was sailing, and they used the log — streamed at intervals — to ascertain the speed of their ship through the water. From this figure they could estimate the distance covered by the ship along the line of her course. The compass was known as early as the twelfth century by the mariners of the Republic of Amalfi, who developed the discovery that a metal needle, magnetised by a lodestone, pointed to the north if left to itself. Stones possessing these magnetising properties were extremely valuable and, like the example below, they were mounted in elaborate and often beautiful settings. The astrolabe is first mentioned in eleventh century chronicles, but seamen did not generally adopt it until a simplified version, called the mariner's astrolabe, was made at the end of the Middle Ages. These methods were, of course, rough in the extreme, but they served the early mariners remarkably well. The log was used for determining longitude for over a thousand years.

21 *above*
The astrolabe, borrowed from the Arabs, was a flattened celestial globe over which was imposed a rotating 'rete' or 'spider' pointing to the Pole Star. It was difficult to make and complicated to use, and it gave only very rough estimates for the observer's latitude. This example, dated 1280, once belonged to Sir Hans Sloane, founder of the British Museum

22 *right*
A Dutch drawing of 1644 illustrating an instrument that had been in use for many centuries. The instructor demonstrates the log, for estimating the speed of a ship through water. In his left hand is the log line attached to a triangular piece of wood, which acts as a drogue in the water when the instrument is streamed astern. The hour-glass times the number of knots in the line as it runs through his fingers

23 *far right*
Lodestones were used for magnetising the needles of ships' compasses. This example, encased in an elaborate silver frame, belonged to Sir George Somers, who founded a settlement in Bermuda in 1609

24
A late medieval round ship jettisons cargo while flying before a gale. The ladders are down, while the good men in the poop pray for help. From a painting by Bicci di Lorenzo

CHAPTER II
Galleys of the Mediterranean

From the days of Imperial Rome until the end of the sixteenth century, sea power in the Mediterranean depended on the galley. Unlike the Viking ships, the galley was carvel-built after the style of the Roman bireme. The old Roman square sail was later discarded in favour of the Moorish lateen rig, a loose-footed triangular sail suspended from a long spar which reached diagonally almost from deck level to a high peak aft, far above the masthead. This sail-plan enabled the galleys to sail much closer to the windward; but they do not appear to have been as well suited to ocean passages as the round ships of the north. A few were built in England but little use was found for them, and of the four great galleys which set sail with the King of Spain's Armada not one reached the English Channel.

Galley battles consisted of top-speed collisions between fleets in line-abreast formation. Each ship would attempt to ram its opponent in some vulnerable quarter, or disable it by shearing off a bank of oars. These opening gambits, followed by hand-to-hand fighting between armed boarding parties, explain the great beaks, or rams, built over the galley's bows. In later times these tactics were rendered even more deadly by the addition of heavy bow guns.

25 *below*
A fifteenth-century pilgrim galley lying off the island of Rhodes, at that time a Christian outpost fortified by Venice. Against surprise attack from the Turkish mainland only a short distance away, a great chain is slung across the heavily defended harbour mouth

26 *above*

The great siege of Valletta, Malta, in 1565, when La Vallette, the Grand Master of the Knights of St John, defended the island against the Turks. The Turkish galleys are at sea, and their camp is shown in the foreground. The Grand Harbour, left, is protected by galleys belonging to the Order

27

A royal prisoner, brother of the Turkish Sultan Djem, is entertained in 1482 by his captors, the Knights Hospitallers of Malta, here distinguished by the cross of their Order

Venice
Queen of the Eastern Mediterranean

The foundations of the powerful Venetian maritime empire were laid during the era of the Crusades. The successive waves of crusading armies which marched eastward from Christian Europe to fight the infidel in the Holy Land needed fleets of troop and baggage transports in unprecedented numbers. The expeditions assembled in the big Mediterranean seaport towns, which served these armies of liberation as supply depots and transit-camps, and willingly built most of their ships for them. Cities such as Amalfi, Pisa, Genoa and Venice drew great wealth from this warlike traffic and construction, and the Republic of Venice grew to be the richest of them all. We know the dimensions (though unfortunately not the numbers) of the galleys she was asked to build for St Louis, who led the eighth and last Crusade of 1268. They were 86 feet long, with a maximum beam of 21 feet and a depth of 22 feet, deep enough to carry two full decks.

28 *above*
A Crusading fleet under Marshal Boucicault in 1399, anchored off the shore of the Holy Land. The overhanging forecastles of these round ships are very prominent

29 *below*
Carpaccio's painting of the legend of St Ursula. The scene, though nominally at Cologne, is laid in any Italian seaport of about 1490. Note the bow-anchor rope which is brought inboard through a hawse-hole

30 *above*
Venice in the sixteenth century, at the height of her sea power. St Mark's and the campanile lie at the entrance to the Grand Canal

31 *below*
The Venetian state galley BUCENTAURE in 1619. In this superbly decorated vessel the Doge and the Senate were rowed out, accompanied by gondolas, to celebrate the marriage between Venice and the sea— a ceremony symbolised by casting a gold ring into the waters

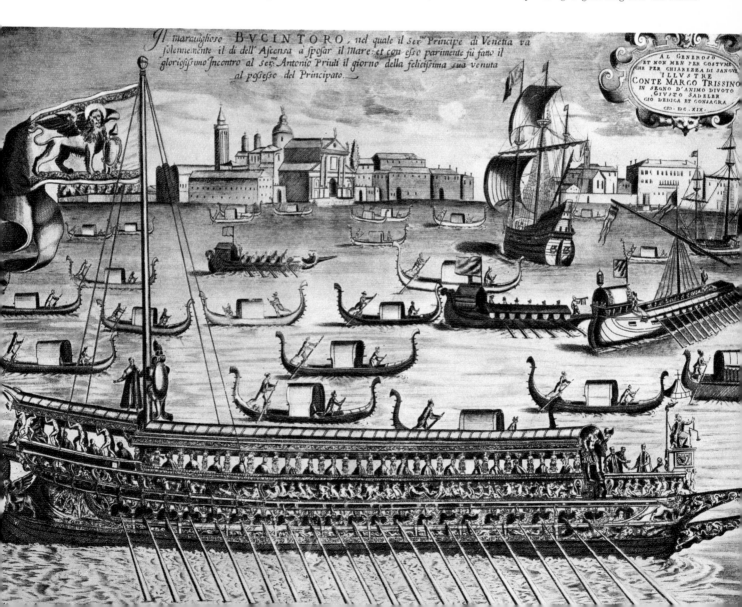

Infidels and Corsairs

32 above
Kheyr-el-din, or Barbarossa, Lord High Admiral of the Ottoman fleet, who led his squadrons against the Christian galleys. He died in 1546, but for centuries thereafter his successors, the Barbary pirates, plundered the Mediterranean from their strongholds on the North African shore, and penetrated even as far as the mouth of the Thames

33 above, right
Algiers in 1630, when the Barbary pirates were at the height of their predatory power. Two Dutch merchantmen and three corsair galleys are fighting it out opposite the town

34 right
The last great battle between galley fleets. In 1571, off the Greek shore at Lepanto, the combined fleets of Christendom under Don John of Austria, met and broke the pride of Turkish sea-power. The picture shows the mêlée once battle had been joined

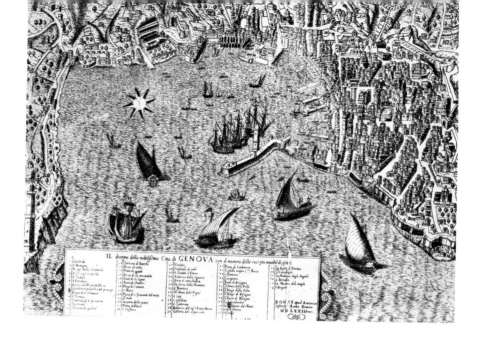

35
At Genoa lateen-rigged galleys lie in the entrance to the port, with larger merchant ships berthed near the mole

36
Andrea Doria of Genoa, the principal Christian admiral in the wars against the Turks between 1530 and 1541

37 *left*

Flagship of the Castilian galley squadron defending the Straits of Gibraltar in the mid-sixteenth century. Note the canopy to protect the galley-slaves during an engagement, the sharp ram which delivered the initial attack in battle, and the soldiers posted on the upper deck ready to board the enemy

38 *below*

An early seventeenth-century galley of the largest size. There were five men to each oar, rowing to the beat of a drum in the stern. The centre gangway was patrolled by overseers who lashed the oarsmen on either side

The Galley Tradition

Compared with the sailing ship, the galley had one great tactical advantage; it was, like the steam-driven warship of later times, a vessel of free movement, independent of wind and tide. In the closed waters of the Mediterranean and in sea battles which were conducted on much the same principles as land battles, this factor was of overwhelming importance. In the end, their lack of broadside firepower, and their instability in the open sea, lost them their long held place among the great battle fleets, even in their native Mediterranean. For patrol duties, coastal work and harbour service, or as convict ships, they were, however, ideal vessels, and they were built and used for these purposes until the end of the eighteenth century.

39 *left*
A French galleasse, so called because she was built on the stouter lines of a round ship which carried guns mounted broadside, and sails as well as oars

40 *above*
A Spanish galley of about 1800 under full sail before the wind. The triangular lateen rig is the origin of all fore-and aft-sails

41 *below*
A sectional drawing of a French merchant galley in 1697. Note the disposition of the cargo below decks

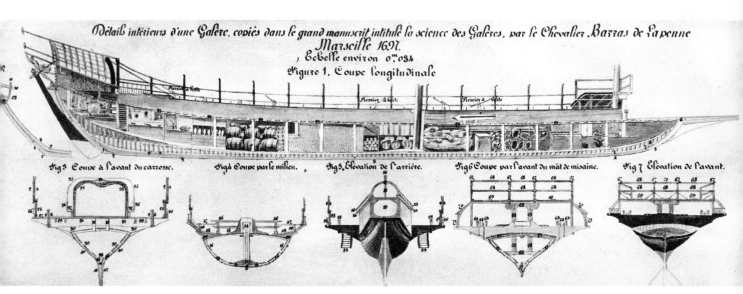

CHAPTER III Spain and Portugal

When Christianity was in its infancy, geographers guessed that the world was round; but their calculations, though not lost, were not generally accessible until the Renaissance, when the body of ancient learning was revived in a Europe which popularly believed that the world was flat. Early in the fifteenth century, after the Ptolemaic maps came to light again and their text was translated into Latin, the picture of the world changed rapidly from the semblance of a tattered pancake to the happier proportions of an orange, and geographers were inspired to seek answers to the great question: What lay on the other side of the world, and how could it be reached?

To the peoples of Italy, Spain and Portugal belong the enduring achievements which answered these questions. To them also we owe the remarkable advances in shipbuilding and navigation, which made possible the great voyages of exploration. There are few pictures, and very little written evidence, to tell us exactly where or how the ships of the Renaissance came to be built. All we know is that the single-masted ship of 1400 had developed by 1450 into the three-masted, and sometimes four-masted, carrack and caravel. They were capable of circumnavigating the world, and were forerunners of the full-rigged ships which were to sail the seas in centuries to come. The *Santa Maria*, and the ships of Magellan, Diaz and Vasco da Gama, were carracks and caravels.

42 above

A geographer of the Renaissance with his compass, lodestone (left foreground), armillary sphere of rings (showing the equator and the tropics), and a quadrant lying beside it. An engraving by Stradanus of Antwerp, early sixteenth century

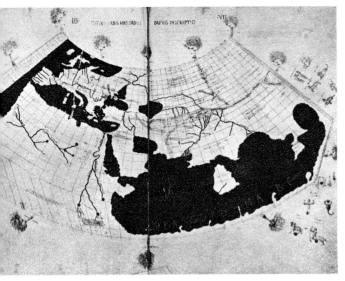

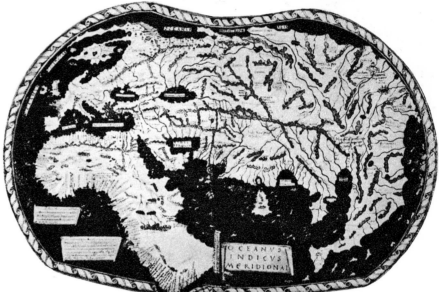

43 *above*
The world according to the Greek geographer Claudius Ptolemy, who lived in Alexandria about 150 A.D. In this Ptolemaic map, from a manuscript of 1475, the prime meridian passes through the Canaries. Owing to the difficulty of ascertaining longitude, the Mediterranean is 65 degrees long instead of 45 degrees

44 *above, right*
The world according to St Beatus, a Spanish monk of the eighth century. Adam, Eve and the serpent are at the top of the Garden of Eden; the Mediterranean is in the centre

45 *right*
A map printed by Martellus Germanus in 1489 shows the world as Columbus conceived it before he sailed. The New World is still missing. Columbus imagined the Far East to be only 3,550 miles west of Europe

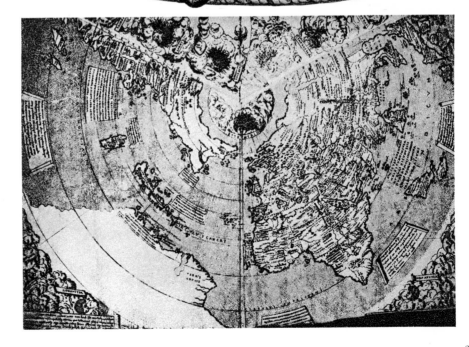

46 *right*
Contarini's map of the world in 1506, the first to show America, though it was not so named until a year later. America is in three parts: north, joined to Cathay; the West Indies, with Japan a little further west; and Terra Crucis, or South America

Henry the Navigator

The expansion of man's knowledge of the world stemmed from the work of Prince Henry of Portugal, or Henry the Navigator, as he came to be called. He saw that a knowledge of navigation was the indispensable key to the unknown lands beyond the featureless horizon. His aim was the discovery of a seaway to India and the East that would turn the flank of Islam and bring the Christian religion to the regions described by Marco Polo. All overland routes were closed by the sword of Islam. There remained the Atlantic, 'the green sea of darkness', uncharted in the memory of man. He took a modest house in the village of Raposeira, not far from Cape St Vincent and the rocky shores of Sagres Bay, and there he collected all that was known or guessed concerning the terrestrial globe, from the works of Ptolemy and Herodotus, to vague legends of Atlantis and the Islands of the Blest. He gathered round him a band of courageous seafarers, and a number of mathematicians, geographers and astronomers. Between them they developed a knowledge of seamanship, of winds and tides and ocean currents and how they could best be used; and a knowledge of navigation — of the sun by day and the stars by night.

Prince Henry sent out his caravels from Sagres Bay to the west, and they discovered Porto Santo, Madeira and the Azores; he sent them south, far beyond Cape Bojador, beyond the burning deserts of Rio de Oro and Cape Blanco, and they found the Cape Verde islands, Gambia, Sierra Leone and the riches of Equatorial Africa. They brought back sea-lion skins, ivory, slaves and gold. But they also brought samples of soil, timber, plants and accurate charts of the places where they had been, and the idea of

47
Sagres Bay and Point, near Cape St Vincent. Here, about a courtyard where the points of the compass are laid out in stone on the ground, there grew up the Vila do Infante — the Prince's town — where Prince Henry of Portugal (1394-1460) taught his sailors the art of navigation

48 *below*
A manuscript map of the world drawn by J. Rotz for Henry VIII, about 1542, showing the results of the voyages of Portuguese and Spanish explorers, who revolutionised man's conception of the globe

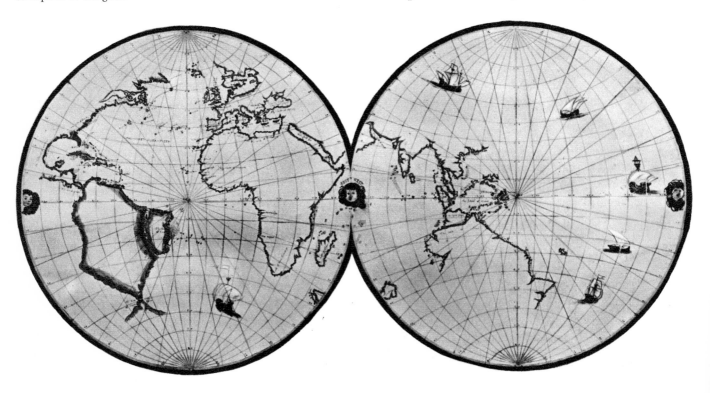

geographical exploration was born. When Prince Henry sent two Portuguese families to Madeira with implements, vine-cuttings, cattle and seed-grain, Europe witnessed the modern world's first colonial enterprise.

The Portuguese, inspired by Prince Henry, became the first traders, explorers, scientists, and missionaries in the new world. In 1488 the caravels of Bartholomew Diaz rounded the Cape of Storms — soon renamed the Cape of Good Hope — and the long-sought route to the East lay open. Herodotus had been right. When Vasco da Gama turned the Cape in 1497 and sailed north to Malindi on the east coast, he took on board an Arab, Majid by name, who piloted the Portuguese ships to Calicut, on the western shore of India. The success of the Portuguese explorers on the Cape route to the East was largely responsible for Columbus' resolve to strike out in the opposite direction and discover a passage westabout to Cathay and the Spice Islands; but the current methods of ascertaining the longitude were so very erratic that he underestimated the distance to Japan by 8,000 miles and discovered the West Indies and Central America instead. He made four voyages to these regions, between 1492 and 1503, and he died in the conviction that he had reached Asia, unaware that he had pioneered the Atlantic route.

Portuguese success continued. In 1500 Cabral and Diaz discovered Brazil by accident, having strayed too far west on their way down the Atlantic to the Cape. On that voyage Bartholomew Diaz died, but the Italian Amerigo Vespucci survived and gave his name to the new-found continent of the south. The greatest voyage of that great age had yet to be made. It began in 1519, when the Portuguese, Ferdinand Magellan, sailed with a fleet of five vessels south down the Atlantic, past the coast of Brazil and South America, and through the southern tropics to the cold high latitudes of the southern

49
A portrait of Prince Henry the Navigator of Portugal, from a detail of a large painting executed by Nuno Gonsalves after Henry's victory over the Moors in 1458. Henry was as much a soldier-crusader as a patron of exploration. Upon his tomb is carved his motto *Talent de bien faire*

50 *above*
A view of Cadiz in 1580, the ancient Gades of Phoenician times. The scene shows fishing for tunny, an important item of diet in Europe

51 *below*
Stradanus, a Flemish Renaissance artist, imagines Noah's construction of the Ark, and takes as his model a ship of his own times

ocean. There he found the Strait which bears his name, and having passed through its tortuous channels, he sailed his ship north-west across the wide Pacific to the Philippines. Among these islands Magellan met his death, and it was left to his first officer, Sebastian del Cano, to bring home the *Victoria*, the only surviving ship. She arrived back at Seville in 1522. Sixty-two years after Prince Henry's death, a ship had circled the globe in the wake of the setting sun. His orders had been obeyed: To reach the furthest point that ever had been touched before, and then to pass beyond.

52

A carrack of about 1470 by the Flemish master
W.A. She had some of the features of the
older round ships, but could carry more cargo.
Her hull was carvel-built, strengthened by
'wales', and her fore- and mizzen-masts were
smaller than in latre developments of the ship

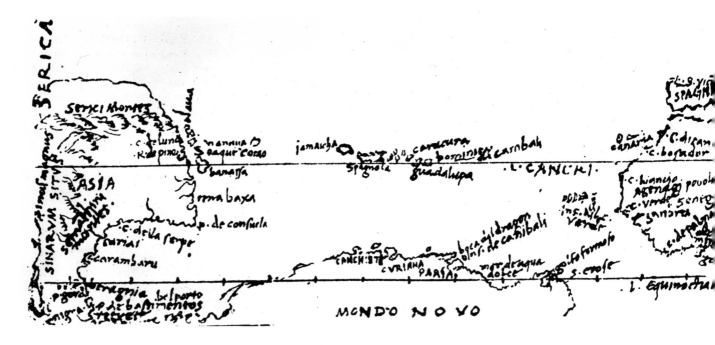

53 *above*
A map said to have been drawn by Columbus' brother, but probably by his friend Zorzi, after Columbus' fourth voyage across the Atlantic in 1502. Asia and South America (*Mondo Novo*) are joined

54 *below*
Columbus lands on an island which he named San Salvador (generally identified with Watling Island in the Bahamas) on 15 October 1492. This is an imaginary reconstruction by de Bry about eighty years later

Christopher Columbus

Columbus was born in Genoa about 1450. He studied the sciences at the University of Pavia, and claimed to have travelled widely from the age of about fourteen. Early in life he convinced himself that the world was a sphere (a notion not popular at the time), and the vision fired him with the desire to reach Asia by a western route. After many trials and errors he persuaded the Spanish crown and court to back his enterprise, and its eventual success brought him fame and riches in the land of his adoption. Thereafter, in the course of a stormy career, when he was alternately in favour and disgrace at court, he made three more voyages to the Indies and America, always firm in the belief that the Asia of his dreams was just around the corner. He had, however, underestimated the size of the world, though he had correctly guessed its shape, and Asia lay ten thousand miles further west.

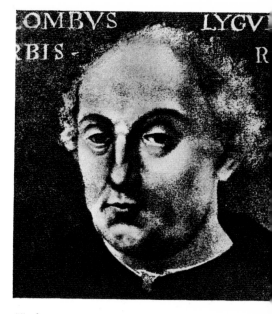

55 *above*
Christopher Columbus (1451-1506). An imaginary portrait at Como by de Orchi. No authentic portrait is known to exist

56 *left*
The SANTA MARIA, Columbus' flagship on his first voyage to the New World, was about 100 tons and square-rigged. She was wrecked off Hispaniola, and forty-four members of her crew, left behind to form the first colony in America, were slaughtered by the natives

57 *below*
The early colonisation of America was accompanied by gruesome incidents of this nature. Within a few years many natives had been exterminated. From de Bry's *America*

Vasco da Gama

Vasco da Gama was born at Sines in the Portuguese province of Alemtejo, probably in the same year that Prince Henry the Navigator died, 1460. He fought as a young man in the wars against Castile, and in a land of great sailors he soon acquired the reputation of being a first class mariner. On 9 July 1497, a fleet of five ships under his command sailed down the River Tagus and out to sea, heading south and west in the wake of Prince Henry's captains. Four months later the Cape of Good Hope was passed in safety, and in the spring of the following year the fleet reached Malindi on the east coast of Africa. From there da Gama struck eastwards across the Arabian Sea and on 20 May he reached Calicut on the Malabar coast. He returned to Lisbon, and for his achievement received from King Manuel I grants of property, rank and income. He made a second successful journey to India, to chastise the Mohammedan elements which were seeking to turn the Hindus against the Portuguese traders. He received the title of Portuguese Admiral of India, and in the reign of King John III was appointed Viceroy. In the same year (1524), only a few months after he had arrived at Goa, he died at Cochin.

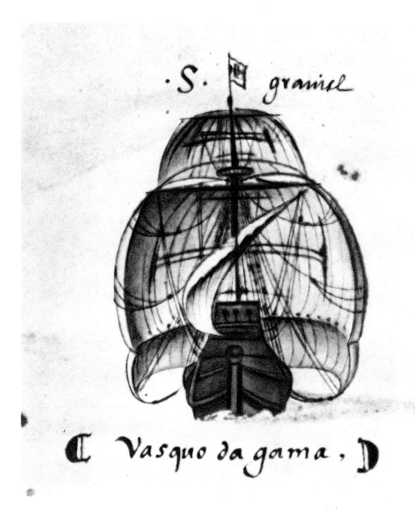

Magellan

Ferdinand Magellan was born at Sabrosa in Portugal about 1480. He was brought up in court as a page to Queen Leonora, and when he was about twenty-four he joined the first viceroy's fleet sailing for India. For the next ten years he travelled widely, fought bravely and was wounded in the service of his country. As a reward he was raised from the ranks of *fidalgos de cotas das armas* (fourth class nobility) to the loftier position of *fidalgo escudeiro*. About this time Magellan fell into disfavour with King Manuel of Portugal and was accused, among other crimes, of trading with the Moors. Later, the charge was dropped, but not before Magellan had renounced his Portuguese nationality and taken his services to the Emperor Charles V and the court of Spain. Here he was well received, and it was from his Spanish patron that he received the authority and financial backing for his great voyage.

60 *above*
Ferdinand Magellan (1480-1521), the first captain to lead an expedition which circumnavigated the world

61 *left*
A woodcut of Magellan's ship, the VICTORIA. The Portuguese ambassador called her one of five 'very old and patched ships', and even the backer of the enterprise said of Magellan, 'I do not count him for much, for he is half crazy'

37

The Development of the Hanseatic Ports

62

A seal from Elbing, dated 1242, illustrating the 'Cog', a new type of ship which originated in northern Europe

63

The seal of Lübeck, another Hanse town, illustrates the rigging of the Cog, which had a single sail hanging from a yard

64 *above*

A type of ship developed in Danzig. The German carpenters used a new method of construction, nailing the planks onto a previously erected framework, and making the stern-rudder a permanent fixture

65 *right*

A drawing by Craemer of the ADLER VON LÜBECK, a later Hanse ship. Lübeck was one of the more important of the Hanse ports, a loose federation of northern free cities formed to promote their commercial interests

66

The JESUS OF LÜBECK, from a manuscript
drawing in the Pepys library at Cambridge.
This ship of the Hanse type was bought by
Henry VIII of England. She was lost to the
Spaniards by Sir John Hawkins in 1567

67

The port of Hamburg in 1497, from a Hamburg
Book of Rights, with Cogs lying in the
Hamburg roads. The port had been in use
since the ninth century, and was an important
link in the Hanse trade

68

Henry VIII of England, whose interest in the sea, ship-building and naval ordnance led to the establishment of a Navy Board which earned for him the title Father of the Royal Navy

69

A 'great ship' of the time of Henry VIII; illustrated in a window of King's College Chapel, Cambridge. She has the high poop and forecastle of the early type of galleon

CHAPTER IV
The Expansion of England

The English were not sea-minded during the Middle Ages. While other nations were annexing oceans, England's naval interests did not extend beyond her coasts. But her merchants had always traded up and down the seaports of the Old World, and they were not pleased to find their ships excluded from the New World by the bulls of a Borgia Pope Alexander VI, a most secular divine, whose pious decrees split the widening world of 1494 between Portugal and Spain, Spain taking all that lay to the west of the 47th meridian and Portugal taking all that lay to the east. Nevertheless, when Englishmen first looked to the open sea, this remarkable division was respected, and their ships sailed away into the bleak unknown north-west. Backed by the royal patronage of King Henry VII (a most able business man) and led by John Cabot and his three sons, Lewis, Sebastian and Sanctus, these early expeditions discovered and formally took possession of Labrador, Newfoundland and the New England coast. But their discoveries were not followed up, and the greatest of them, Sebastian, took service at the Court of Spain.

Henry VIII built ships to impress the French, like the *Great Harry*, (see overleaf), and founded the Royal Navy. But he was more concerned with his domestic affairs than with mounting distant expeditions, and English

continued on page 44

70
Brueghel's masterly representation of an early
sixteenth-century ship, a galleon with four
masts and a high stern

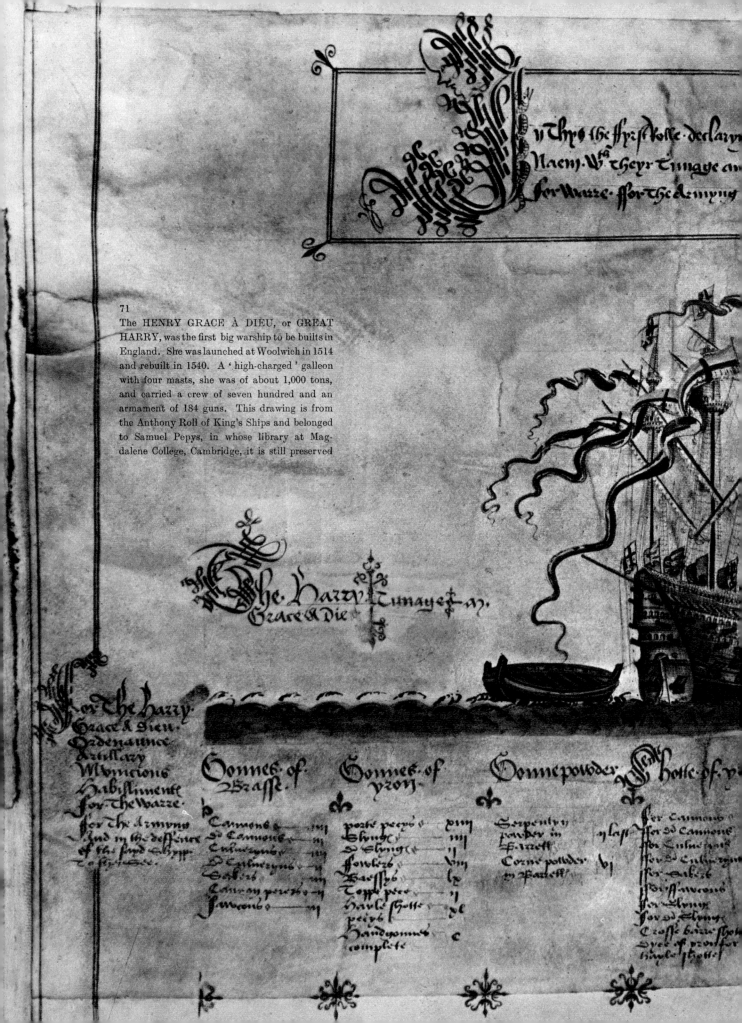

71

The HENRY GRACE À DIEU, or GREAT HARRY, was the first big warship to be built in England. She was launched at Woolwich in 1514 and rebuilt in 1540. A 'high-charged' galleon with four masts, she was of about 1,000 tons, and carried a crew of seven hundred and an armament of 184 guns. This drawing is from the Anthony Roll of King's Ships and belonged to Samuel Pepys, in whose library at Magdalene College, Cambridge, it is still preserved

...mbre of the kyngs Maiesties owne Shyppes wth euze Shyppe and Chyrgs
...of men. As Also the ordenaunce Artillary & Monicions and Habillement
...ce of euery of the sayd Shyppes Agaynst theyr enemyes vppon the See.

What ys to Saye

Men

Souldiours	ccclx
marynars	ccc
Gonnars	cl

Gonnes of Iron and Leade · Bowes Bowestrynge Arrowes Moryspyckes Byllys Dartes for toppys · Monicions · Habillements for the

Gonnes of Iron and leade		Bowes Bowestrynge Arrowes Morys pykes Byllys Dartes for toppys		Monicions		Habillements for the	
Canon peces	lx	Bowes of yews	vc	prkthamers	xx	Ropis of hempe for	
porte peces	ccc	Bowestrynge	xgred	Heddys of yron	vy	anchors & slynings	
Sakers	c	Lyuere Arrowes	byel	Crowes of yron	vy	Barlis of sundre sort	
Toppe peces	xl	in shedys		Comaunders	xij	Barys of Iedd	
Fawcons	xxyj	Morys pykes	cc	Tampions	vdc	ffrrkins & pycsin	
... of leade		Byllys	cc	Caulas for		... part	
handgonnes	xyd	Dartes for toppys	jc	Cartowches	xxhdyo	Ipar whete	
... of leade	xyb	in coffens		paper riall		Ipar tonckas	
				for cartowches		Iper pypys	
				fommes for	vj	Ikpe stauus	
				cartowches		Tomber for fablys	

72
Bound for his meeting in June 1520 with the French king, Francis I, at the Field of the Cloth of Gold, Henry VIII embarks at Dover in the GREAT HARRY. Her four masts, from right to left, are fore, main, mizzen and bonaventure mizzen, of which the latter two are lateen-, or triangular-, rigged. She is also rigged for topgallants. A contemporary painting by Holbein

continued from page 40

exploration languished. His son, Edward VI, did nothing to revive it. In the same year that Mary Tudor came to the throne, Sebastian Cabot returned to England, and his theories of a northern passage to Cathay inspired Willoughby and Chancellor to sail north-east in search of it.

It was now the fifth decade of the sixteenth century. Some twenty years earlier, a Frenchman, Jacques Cartier, had sailed up the St Lawrence River and founded New France. The English, misled by the geographer Mercator, began their stubborn search for a north-west passage to Cathay, a wild goose chase signposted with brave deeds and illustrious names. The Iberian nations were still secure in the tropical worlds that they had discovered, but the tide of events was beginning to turn against them.

Far apart, off the glittering islands of the Indies east and west, the Spaniards and Portuguese had ruled for half a century and more, undisturbed by the sight of an English flag or the sound of an English gun. Soon their fortunes in these distant regions were to suffer a change from which they have never recovered.

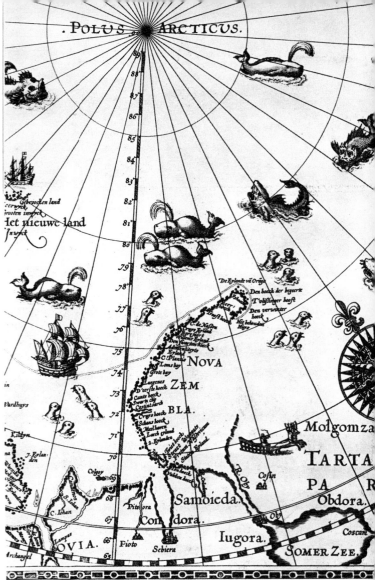

73 *above, left*
Sebastian Cabot (1470-1555), of Genoese origin, first served under Henry VII, and later under the kings of Spain. He returned to England and inspired the first voyages of exploration to the north-east in the reign of Edward VI

74 *above*
A map of 1598, illustrating the search for a north-east passage. The Dutch navigator, Willem Barents, made three voyages between 1594 and 1597 in an attempt to find a way round Novaya Zemlya (Nova Zembla), and in the last voyage he perished in the ice

75 *left*
A merchant ship of 1530, by Holbein. The passengers and crew are clearly in a cheerful mood, freely drinking in the bows, while flagons of ale are passed up to the men in the crow's-nest

76 *above*

A shipwright measures the lines of a blue-print before transferring them to the floor of the moulding loft, where the timbers of a ship were cut.

77 *below*

'Drake's Dial', a unique miniature aid to navigation, made by Humphrey Cole in 1569. It combined, in one instrument, a compass, a quadrant, tables of latitude and tide-tables

Sir John Hawkins

While the search went on in the bitter north, the Hawkins family of Plymouth had been pioneering a more promising and warmer route to riches. Before Elizabeth I came to the throne, William Hawkins had begun to trade regularly to the Guinea coast for ivory. His son John, born in 1532, followed early in his father's wake; but instead of exporting ivory, he exported natives of West Africa and sold them into slavery in the West Indies. Inevitably he fell foul of the Spaniards there. But John Hawkins and others like him were not impressed by papal bulls or Spanish threats. He knew where he could get doubloons, and in his eyes the man who got them had the title to them. At the outset, he was no better than an armed smuggler. Undoubtedly rude, and probably greedy, his soul was not above fraud; but he was brave enough to defy the might of Spain, and he led the way in questioning her pretensions to a trade monopoly in the New World. In the course of time, he rose to be the principal administrative officer of the Queen's Navy, and he cared well for her ships. He also rendered his country a signal service by giving a young relative of his a chance to sail across the Atlantic. The youth's name was Francis Drake.

78 *above*
Sir John Hawkins (1532-95), merchant adventurer, slaver and admiral. He provoked the Spaniards with almost every voyage he undertook, and filled his pockets at their expense. Later he became treasurer of the English navy, and built and armed the ships which defeated the Armada

79 *below*
The GRIFFIN, which fought against the Spanish Armada, was an older type of galleon with a high poop and low beakhead. The illustration dates from the Armada year, 1588

47

80 *above*

An incident on Drake's voyage round the world (1577-80) when he landed in Patagonia, South America, and the natives snatched the cap from his head. The artist de Bry engraved this picture for his history of America a few years later

81

Part of a map made by Jacob Hondius in honour of the voyages of Drake and Cavendish, and containing at the foot the only known picture of the GOLDEN HIND

Sir Francis Drake

The seamen of Drake's generation looked upon war with Spain as a religious duty, a national privilege and a steady source of hard currency. In his early twenties, Drake fought in the Gulf of Mexico under John Hawkins, and before he was thirty he led an expedition of three ships which took and plundered the Spanish town of Nombre de Dios. He penetrated inland across the Isthmus of Panama, and from the branches of a tree, he got his first glimpse of the Pacific Ocean and resolved to 'sail an English ship in these seas'. He then returned to Nombre de Dios, filled his ships with plunder from the town, and sailed for England. In 1577 he departed south and west again with five ships manned by 166 men. Thirty-four months later he entered Plymouth with one ship, the *Golden Hind*, and a small company of survivors with whom he had circumnavigated the world. At Deptford the Queen visited his ship and conferred a knighthood upon him.

82
Sir Francis Drake (1540-96) was both privateer and naval officer. He was the first man to take his own ship around the world, and he played the principal part in the war against Spain

83
A modern model of the GOLDEN HIND, now at Plymouth, Devon. No certain details of her build have survived, but it has been estimated that she was a vessel of about 100 tons, 90 foot long, 19 foot beam, armed with fourteen guns and crewed by 160 men and boys

84 *left*
The ARK ROYAL, Howard's flagship, was built by Richard Chapman for Sir Walter Raleigh, who sold her to the Crown.

85
Queen Elizabeth, from a medal struck after the defeat of the Spanish Armada

86
Sir Walter Raleigh (1552-1618), courtier, seaman, soldier, explorer, poet, scientist and historian — the ideal of Elizabethan manhood. He was executed at the Tower of London, in spite of all his qualities and services to his country

87 *left*

Howard of Effingham (1536-1624), Lord Admiral of England and commander-in-chief of the English fleet which defeated the Spanish Armada. Like the Spanish commander, the Duke of Medina Sidonia, he was of noble birth and a great courtier rather than a seaman

88 *right*

Sir Martin Frobisher (1535-94), an intrepid seaman and a hot-tempered man, explored the icy seas of the North-West Passage, and quarreled violently with his compatriots in warmer latitudes

89 *below*

The Spanish Armada off Plymouth on 21 July 1588. The English fleet was obliged to move out of Plymouth against a head-wind, and then split into two squadrons, one of which tacked WSW along the coast to take position behind the Spaniards, while the other sailed SSW across the Armada's van

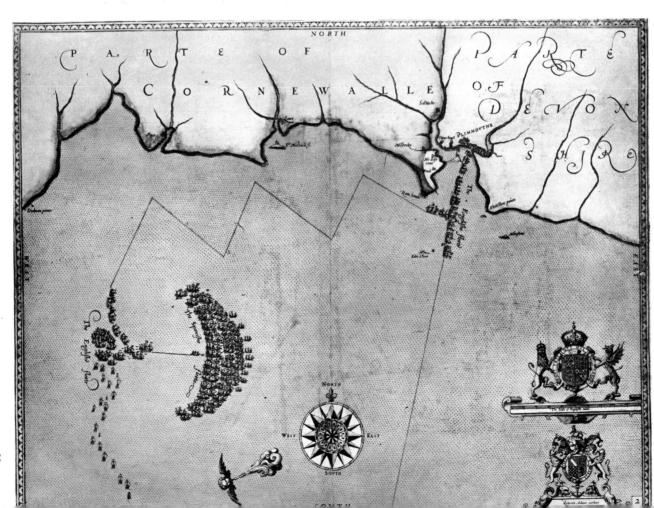

The Armada

Spain sought revenge on the English captains. She mustered in Lisbon and in Cadiz bay a great fleet, a great army and much ordnance for the purpose. Hearing of these sinister preparations, Drake sailed into Cadiz bay on 19 April 1587 and fired upwards of 10,000 tons of Spanish shipping. Nevertheless, in May of the following year, the Spanish Armada sailed north under the Duke of Medina Sidonia. The fleet was one of 130 ships manned by 30,000 men and mounting 2,500 guns. The seamen of England gathered under Lord Howard of Effingham to meet it. They mustered 102 ships. The squadron commanders were Hawkins, Drake, Frobisher, with Seymour in the Thames. The Armada was sighted off the Lizard on the evening of 19 July. That night the English fleet put out from Plymouth. Outgunned and outsailed, the noble Spanish commanders fought their way up-Channel with courage, but they lacked experience of the narrow seas, and fortune was against them. They lost heavily to the English, but more heavily and more tragically still on their long storm-racked voyage home. England lost not a single ship and less than a hundred men. Of the Invincible Armada, only about sixty-five ships returned to Spanish ports. Victory was complete, and England emerged from the struggle a first class sea power.

91
The medal struck to commemorate the defeat of the Armada. The Latin inscription reads, 'God blew, and they were dispersed. 1588'

90 *below*
The two actions off Portland and the Isle of Wight, which took place on 23 and 25 July. Frobisher's squadron is on the English left, inshore; Drake is on the right; and Howard and Hawkins in the centre. These two charts were made by William Adams and John Ryther in the same year as the battle

53

92

The voyage of Barents, the Dutchman, to discover the North-East Passage in 1596. The hut where he spent the winter was found in 1871, and part of Barents' journal within it. Most of his crew survived by escaping in open boats, but Barents himself died of exhaustion on 30 June 1597

93

Barents' ship, separated from her companion ship, made her way through the ice-floes for some distance, but then became inextricably caught in the ice after rounding Novaya Zemlya

94

Barents' encounter with a polar bear. These three illustrations come from Spilbergen's contemporary account of the voyage

The first colonies

Warfare, exploration and trade by sea spread round the world, financed by the chartered companies of English merchant adventurers — the Muscovy, Levant, Guinea, Hudson's Bay and the East India companies. Sir Walter Raleigh, Sir Humphrey Gilbert and Captain John Smith pursued their schemes for founding English colonies on the Atlantic seaboard of America. Portugal and Spain, united now under one crown, still sought to pursue their monopoly of the produce of the Indies, but the English and the Dutch thought otherwise. They wanted to bring home the spices themselves. Their aim was achieved in two ways: they went long voyages to the East to obtain the spices, or, with far less trouble to themselves, they let the Spaniards do all the hard voyaging and captured their great lumbering carracks nearer home. The *Madre de Dios, San Felipe, San Valentino*, to mention a very rich few, were taken in this way. Ships improved, however, as well as gunnery, and soon the English and the Dutch were sailing regularly to the East, to be followed by the French, and warfare smouldered among the islands. The handful of men who had brought glory to England, and won for her ships their freedom on the oceans, were going to their graves. Hawkins had died off Porto Rico in 1595, and, a few weeks later, Drake met his death in Nombre de Dios Bay. The Elizabethans and their ships were vanishing. They have no better epitaph than the words of their Admiral who defeated the Armada: 'God send us to sea in such a company again, when need be'.

95 above
Sir Humphrey Gilbert, coloniser of Newfoundland and one of the first explorers of the North-West Passage. His last words, shouted to his consort, the HIND, as his ship was foundering in an Atlantic gale, were, 'We are as near to heaven by sea as by land'

96 below
'The arrival of the Englishmen in Virginia' — a sketch by John White, one of the original settlers of Roanoke in 1585

The Great New World

97
Captain John Smith, first governor of Virginia,
founder in 1607 of Jamestown

98 *below*
A model of the MAYFLOWER, made by Dr
R.C. Anderson in 1926, and now in Pilgrims'
Hall, Plymouth, Mass. It is based on the
best available evidence, although no drawings
of the ship of 1620 have survived, and it was
used in the reconstruction of the MAYFLOW-
ER in which Commander Alan Villiers sailed
across the Atlantic in 1957

99 *above*

A Dutch traveller's impression of South America in 1596. The pearl divers and the fishing cormorant are credible, but the creature on the right, one of Othello's 'anthropophagi, whose heads do grow beneath their shoulders', is not of that, or any other, world

100 *below*

The most important export from America was codfish, caught off Newfoundland by the English and the French. A French drawing of 1698

The Expansion of Trade

101 *right*
St Helena, a vital watering place on the route to the south, was originally a Portuguese and Dutch base, and became British in 1659

102 *below*
Houtman's Anglo-Dutch fleet rounding the Cape of Good Hope in 1596. The Cape was settled by the Dutch as a halfway house to India, until it was captured by the British in 1796

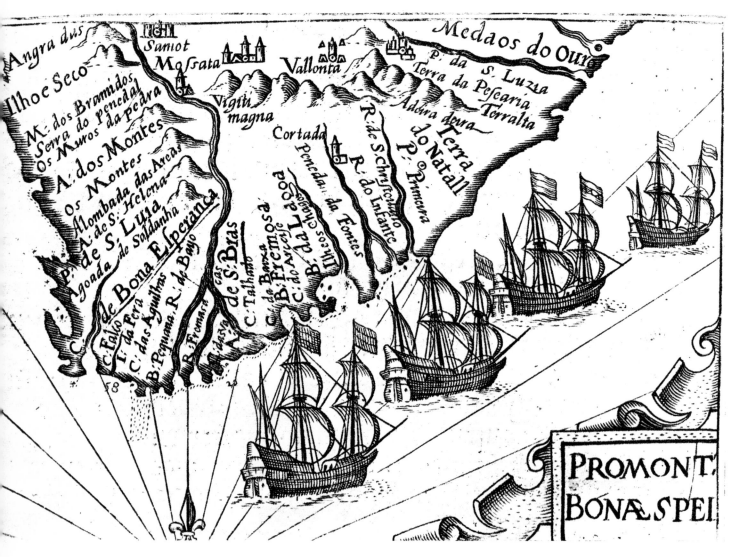

francois.

A. Misericordia

Sande Poortbryder

Joannes a'Doetechum fecit

Congesta huc videas Ganges quæ portat et Indus / Insulæ et Eoo maxima in Oceano. / Ploxerb.

Fori Goensis tabernarum mercium et mer / catorum illud frequentantium aperta ex / plicatio per N. Linschoten.

Clare opdoeninge vande merckt van Goa / met haer winckelen waren en dagelickse / Coophyeden door I. H. V. Linschoten.

44 en 45

103 *left*

The Portuguese settlement at Goa in 1599, from Linschoten's *Itinerary*. An already advanced state of civilisation is indicated by this illustration

104 *below*

Bantam in Java, where Dutch and English merchants traded Javanese pepper for Chinese silks, until the English were ousted in 1616

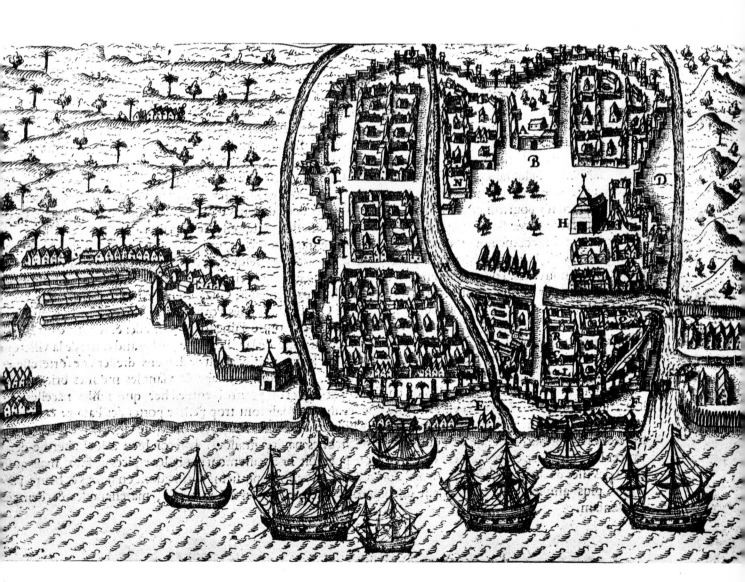

Rivals to English Sea-Power

106 *above*
A Portuguese carrack or East Indiaman of the early sixteenth century. Attributed to C. Anthoniszoon, 1521

105 *left*
A Dutch ship of 1565 by Pieter Brueghel. She was a multi-decked warship with forecastle set further back than in the old carracks. Her armament was ten heavy, fourteen medium and thirty small guns

107 *right*
An illustration by Brueghel to the story of Icarus and Daedalus. The ship had a much deeper waist than usual, more like a galleon

De Kraeck Ste Tso mo
Van

DE STRAET

VAN MALACKE

108
A battle in the Malacca Strait in 1602. The
three Dutch ships in the foreground, and the
three English ships beyond, combine to attack
a huge Portuguese carrack in circumstances
most favourable to the allies, since the wind
appears to be blowing from all quarters at
once. When the Portuguese had been driven
out of the Indies, the Dutch and English
fought each other for the spice monopoly,
until the English settled for India

109

Title-page of the first printed book of sea-charts, translated from the Dutch of Lucius
Waghenaer, and published in England in 1588. *The Mariner's Mirror*, the quarterly journal
of the Society of Nautical Research, is still issued under the same cover

CHAPTER V
Triumph of the Dutch

If any race may rightfully claim mastery of the sea, it is the Dutch. They raised their land from under it, they built their cities in it, and they drew their wealth from its uttermost limits; at one time or another they defeated every nation of any consequence during their long struggle to win independence from Spain, a struggle in which the English were at first disposed to help them, though it is hard to say whether Leicester's manoeuvres in the Low Countries were a help or hindrance to the cause. Nevertheless, in the face of much adversity, the Dutch forged ahead. The independence of the Seven United Provinces was recognised in 1596, and within a few years the Dutch were collecting the freighting profits of all Europe as well as most of the herring in the North Sea.

Freight and fish were the foundations of their prosperity, and it grew apace. Their East India Company was formed in 1602, and twenty years later a separate company was formed to exploit the wealth of the West Indies. An Englishman of the time wrote: ' The prodigious increase of the Netherlands in their domestic and foreign trade, riches, and multitude of shipping is the envy of the present age. ' He was not exaggerating. In a few decades the Dutch had freed themselves from the millstone of the Spanish Crown and turning upon the broad dominions of their former masters they won a seaward empire that stretched from Spitzbergen to the Cape of Good Hope, and from Central America to the Spice Islands, via the west coast of Africa. Their methods of conquest were crude, even by the standards of those days.

110 *below*
A Dutch cargo barge of 1580, rigged with a loose-footed foresail (a rig still carried by Thames barges), and trailing overboard, the leeboard. Line engraving by Visscher

111 *below*
The 'Four Days Battle', an action fought in June 1666 between the Duke of Albemarle and de Ruyter, from which the Dutchman emerged victorious. The English flagship, ROYAL CHARLES, is on the right of this painting by Abraham Storck; de Ruyter's flagship, the ZEVEN PROVINCIEN, lies in the centre

112
Martin Tromp (1597-1653) defeated a Spanish fleet in the Channel in 1639. A story is told that he sailed up the English Channel with a broom at his masthead to indicate his ability to sweep the seas. He was killed in action against Cromwell's navy in July 1653

113
Cornelius Tromp (1629-91), son of Martin, commanded with de Ruyter in the second and third Anglo-Dutch wars. By Sir Peter Lely

114
Robert Blake (1599-1657), ranking in esteem only after Nelson and Drake in the long line of English admirals, did not go to sea until the age of fifty. Under his command, the Royal Navy defeated the Dutch and Spanish

115 *right*
Michel de Ruyter (1607-76), the greatest seaman of his age, was victorious against the English and Spanish, both in the Mediterranean and the Channel

116 *below*
A Dutch fleet, led by de Ruyter, sailing up the River Medway in 1667. He fired most of the English fleet as it lay at anchor, and cut adrift the flagship ROYAL CHARLES, which he towed back to Amsterdam, where her stern is exhibited to this day near de Ruyter's tomb

The Anglo-Dutch Wars

Strangely enough, it was a fellow republican, Oliver Cromwell, who first brought the English into conflict with the Dutch at sea. The causes underlying the outbreak of hostilities were manifold: jealousy of Dutch trade which was prospering unchecked in Europe and the east, the large English navy, well equipped and manned to fight the Royalists, and certainly Cromwell's Navigation Act, which forbade imports except in English ships. At all events, the naval engagements which followed were tumultuous and bloody. They continued, at intervals, for about thirty years. Both sides were led by brilliant and courageous seamen and both sides suffered heavy losses, as first the Dutch and then the English wrested satisfying victories from each other. Tactics and strategy improved, ship-construction was modified and refined, and out of the mêlée there emerged the line-of-battle ship, the regular man-of-war, at last entirely distinct from the armed merchantmen and cargo.

Thanks to the work of two of the best war artists of the time, the Van de Veldes (father and son), we know a great deal about both the Dutch and English ships of this period, for the Van de Veldes were invited to sketch the ships of England as well as those of her foes.

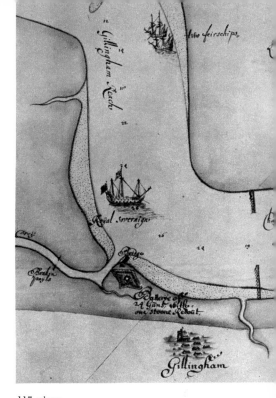

117 *above*
A chart of the Medway in 1667, showing the battery which prevented the Dutch from attacking the ROYAL SOVEREIGN

119 *below*
The ROYAL CHARLES (ex-NASEBY) sketched by Van de Velde, who became the official marine artist to both sides in the Anglo-Dutch wars.

118 *below*
De Ruyter's flagship, the ZEVEN PROVIN-CIEN, drawn with a minute accuracy of detail by W. van de Velde

120

The SOVEREIGN OF THE SEAS of 1637, probably the most beautiful ship ever built in England. She was the first three-decker of a hundred guns, with three masts and rigged for royals above the top-gallant sails. She was designed by Peter and Phineas Pett, and paid for out of the Ship Money tax. A contemporary engraving by John Payne

Samuel Pepys

121
Samuel Pepys (1633-1703), the Secretary to the Admiralty and chief administrator of the Navy in the reigns of Charles II and James II. Many of the ships' models and pictures in this volume come from his collection

Samuel Pepys was not only the most famous diarist of the seventeenth century, but a most efficient Secretary of the Admiralty. He inherited not only Cromwell's ships, but also the cost of building them, and throughout the reign of Charles II he had to struggle to find the means of keeping the fleet at sea. That England had a navy at all during the Dutch wars was largely due to his efforts.

His reforms in naval administration had a lasting effect. He waged continual war against slack discipline, incompetent commanders and dishonest contractors. He tried to make officers worthy of their trust and to see that the men were well paid and well fed. That he did not always succeed was not his fault. Realising the incompetence of 'gentlemen' captains and the shortcomings of 'tarpaulin' seamen bred only to the sea, he virtually founded the naval profession by instituting a technical examination for all lieutenants. He also insisted that chaplains, surgeons and schoolmasters should be carried on board all large ships.

A man of wide interests, he was President of the Royal Society, Master of Trinity House and a notable patron of navigation, cartography and astronomy. His library is still preserved at his old college at Cambridge in the glass-fronted bookcases which he invented. He was instrumental in founding the Royal Observatory at Greenwich for the purpose of discovering a means of finding the longitude, and it was under his auspices that the first official charts were made of the coasts surrounding Britain.

122 *left*
Hadley's octant (1732) an instrument for finding the latitude soon to become the sextant. Its inventor claimed, ' With this instrument, though the ship rolls ever so much, yet the image of any object will remain absolutely immovable '

123 *above*
Gunter's quadrant (1676), an instrument by which the altitude of the sun or a star could be measured by locating it through a sight attached to the plumb line

124 *left*
The PRINCE (1670) one of the finest models in the collection of Samuel Pepys. Designed by the great shipwright Phineas Pett, she was a line-of-battle ship with three decks

125 *above*
Sir Jeremy Smith, a professional sea-captain, attained flag rank under Pepys, whose reforms ensured that all captains were competent officers, whether they were gentlemen or not

126 *above*
The earliest surviving marine telescope, made of wood and parchment. The owner's name, Jacob Cunigham, and the date of manufacture (1661) are engraved on the decorated lens cap

127 *right*
A student of navigation using a backstaff in 1681. With his back to the sun, he shoots its reflection in a mirror sight, thereby determining its altitude, and after much calculation, his own latitude

128 *above*

A view of Stockholm in 1680, the Baltic port from which came most of the timber and hemp used in the Dutch and English navies. Under Queen Christina's rule, a powerful Swedish navy dominated the Baltic

129 *below*

Amsterdam at the height of her glory in 1660. The harbour-master's tower (left centre), where Dutch women went for news of their menfolk, was then known as the Wailing Tower. It still survives

Ships at Peace

130
Dutch warships close inshore, the lower gun ports open and the guns run out. The ship
on the left is de Ruyter's. All big ships were by then three-masted, and there was a greater
tendency towards flush decks and a highly ornamental stern

The Dutch Merchantmen

A shipping company which could bring the spices of the East to the markets of Europe was assured of a handsome profit, but in those days the round trip lasted six months or more, and there were considerable problems to be solved before the profits could be touched. Merchant ships had to carry bigger cargoes (to make the long voyage pay), greater armament (to deal with well-armed foes), more sail (to drive the heavier hulls), and they required friendly ports of call along the way. In answer to these needs a new class of ship, the East Indiamen, appeared upon the seas to succeed the carrack — bigger than any other merchantmen of those times — and along the Cape route to the East there grew up a chain of ports where these vessels could refill their water butts, replenish their galley bunkers, and feed their scurvy-ridden crews on fresh fruit and vegetables. The English, the French and the Dutch invested in the construction of these big, armed merchant ships, and sailed to the East to capture the spice trade from the Spaniards

131 *above*
The yacht PORTSMOUTH, named by Charles II after his mistress the Duchess of Portsmouth, and built by Phineas Pett on the lines of a Dutch yacht. Yachts had been armed vessels until that date

and the Portuguese. At the outset the three northern nations joined forces in a common effort to drive their Iberian predecessors from the island sea. But as soon as their task was accomplished the Dutch turned upon their French and English allies. They had, moreover, in their energetic wisdom, colonised and garrisoned many of the watering places along the route, and very soon it became clear that the Dutch were now masters of the Spice Islands. From their bases there they pushed north to insular Japan, and for many years the Dutch were the only European traders against whom the Japanese ports were not firmly closed. Driven from the richest field by a power superior to their own, the English turned reluctantly to India, where the Dutch did not molest them unduly. There the East India Company, which had been formed in 1601 with a capital of £ 72,000, set up its factories again and sent its agents in search of trade. Dazzling returns were to be won from this small investment; but at the start the company operated in a small way, unaware of its advantageous situation.

133 *below*
The JUPITER, a Dutch East Indiaman, from an engraving by C.J. Visscher, 1626. She had the low projecting beakhead of the period, and was as heavily armed as a warship

132 *above*
A yacht used by the Dutch as a convoy cruiser, 1660. The leeboard allowed a ship of shallow draft to beat to windward

Dutch Shipbuilders

134 *right*
A Dutch galleon of 1629, with a square sprit-sail below the bowsprit to keep the head of the ship before the wind

135
The construction of a new East Indiaman, about 1640. On the right a ship is careened to be tarred and caulked below the water line. Etching by Hollar

136
A scene in a Dutch ship-yard, from Van Yk's
manual on naval architecture, 1697

CHAPTER VI
The French Navy and its Rivals

While the Dutch and the English were burning and sinking each other's fleets in different parts of the world, France was under the iron hand of Jean Baptiste Colbert. His aims were power, prestige and prosperity for France, and his argument was simple: France would not be proud or powerful until all other nations were beggared. Louis XIV was anxious to fight on dry land; but in Colbert's view, the chief obstacles were the sea powers of Holland and England, and he planned for their downfall with a fixity of purpose that earned him, from Madame de Sévigné, the sobriquet ' the North Star '. The result of his endeavours was the French Royal Navy, a mighty force of splendid ships with which he hoped to sweep rival powers from the seas. During the last of the Anglo-Dutch wars his navy skirmished on the English side, but Colbert had built it with an eye to protecting French commerce and encouraging French colonial expansion. On the whole he therefore kept his powder dry. He did not wish to risk his ships in European squabbles while French trade and French territories abroad lagged far behind the Dutch

137 *opposite*
A detail from Claude Lorrain's *Embarkation of St Ursula*, about 1646, illustrating a merchant vessel of the period. Note the stern-walk for the captain and his family

138 *above*
LE GRAND ST LOUIS, flagship of the French navy (1640), annotated with the terms then in use for the different parts of a ship and her rigging

139 *above*
The Comte de Tourville, the finest tactician
to serve in the French navy. He defeated
the English off Beachy Head in 1690, but
his fleet was destroyed by an Anglo-Dutch
fleet under Admiral Russell in 1692

and English enterprises. Fortunately for him, he did not live to see the
defeat of his cherished marine.

When the Popish James II fled from a Protestant England, leaving his
crown to be jointly donned by William of Orange and Mary, he went to
France where Louis XIV offered to help him to reconquer his realm. At
first, they were successful. Colbert's navy, under the Admiral the Comte
de Tourville, defeated the combined fleets of England and Holland off Beachy
Head; but Tourville did not drive home his victory as he might have done.
James II was beaten in Ireland, and William and Mary held the island. Two
years later, in 1692, a second invasion was attempted. Tourville, with a
fleet of 44 ships of the line, was sent to clear the Channel for the
invading armies. The Allied fleet, anchored off Spithead, numbered 63
English ships and 36 Dutch ships, under the command of Admiral Edward
Russell. The battle of Barfleur-La Hogue, as it was clumsily called,
lasted for five days. Tourville fought skilfully, but the odds were
overwhelmingly against him. The French lost fifteen ships including Tourville's flagship *Soleil Royal*, and most of her army transports were
burned at their moorings in the bay of La Hogue. James II lost his final
chance of recapturing his throne; and Louis XIV expressed his firm prefer-
ence for feats of arms upon the good earth of Europe.

The wars of William and his successor Anne dragged on uncompromisingly
on shore and afloat until the Treaty of Utrecht was signed in 1713. By then,
England was supreme both in the Mediterranean and the Atlantic.

140 *left*
The battle of Barfleur-La Hogue, painted by
the Dutch artist, A. Salm. Tourville's flagship, SOLEIL ROYAL, is being engaged on
the left; she was later beached and burned
on the Cherbourg peninsula

141 *right*
The RESOLUTION in a gale, a masterpiece
by Van de Velde painted in the reign of
Charles II. It gives an excellent idea of the
ornamental sterns then in fashion. The upper
tier of gun ports are open, but the lower tier
are closed on account of the high seas

142
Jean Baptiste Colbert (1619-83), Louis XIV's Minister of Marine, who founded the naval and colonial power of France, but failed to persuade his royal master that the destiny of France lay on the sea rather than upon land

143 *below*
Stern view of a French two-decker in Louis XIV's navy. Moored fore and aft, she lies beam-on to a steady breeze, her gun ports open and her sails neatly furled

144 *below, right*
Bows of the SOLEIL ROYAL, the French flagship burned at La Hogue in 1692

Colbert's Navy

The methods by which Colbert created a French Royal Navy were far-reaching. In 1669 he was appointed Minister of Marine by Louis XIV, who was more interested in the army and its exploits under Louvois and Vauban, and he set himself the task of reviving and extending the colonial empire of France. He settled the first French factories in India, acquired possessions in Guiana for the French Crown, established outposts in Madagascar; while La Salle, with Colbert's support, extended the frontiers of New France from Canada to the Mississippi. To protect these colonies, Colbert built magnificent ships, and fortified for their use the harbours of Toulon, Rochefort, Havre, Brest and Dunkirk. He founded naval schools in several of these ports, and introduced a system of naval conscription which remained virtually unchanged until the twentieth century. Recruits served for six months every three, four or five years, according to their merit as seamen, and for three months after service they received half-pay. Pensions were introduced, corruption was stamped out of the civil administration, and everything possible was done to make the service attractive.

Colbert's methods of recruitment for the Mediterranean galleys (a system inherited from the past) were not so pretty. Oarsmen were needed at the benches, but as it was a job for which no sane man would apply, Colbert wrote to the judges of France and requested them to sentence for service in the galleys as many muscular miscreants who came their way. Tramps, smugglers, political rebels, minor criminals and burglars were sent to man the galleys, beside Negro slaves and Iroquois Indians deported from New France, and once chained to the oars, they had little hope of release, since the term of the sentence was apt to be forgotten by the authorities.

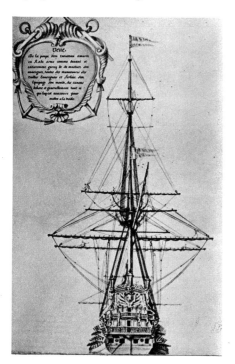

145 *above*

A two-decker from *Mr Dummer's draughts of the body of an English man-of-war*, a work compiled for Samuel Pepys

146 *left*

Section of a French three-decker of 1698, from Tourville's manual of fleet instructions. Water and provision casks are stowed above the gravel ballast

147 *below*

Detail of an entry-port in the topsides of a Swedish warship. From a Swedish model of 1682

Ship-building

During the latter part of the seventeenth century there were marked advances in the design of ships and the techniques of building them. Builders' models and draughtsmen's plans have survived from the period, and they tell us a great deal about the methods then in use. When a ship was to be built, a scale model of her was first made. If it met with the customer's approval, the lines of the ship were taken direct from the model or blue-print, and worked up to full scale on the floor of the moulding-loft.

148 *above*
A rigged model of the 60-gun DREAD-NOUGHT, a vessel of 1704, ornamented in the baroque style. She was 907 tons burden. The planks are cut away below the water line to show the construction of the hull

149 *below, right*
When a ship was to be built, the timber contractor placed wooden templates against the tree-trunks, to determine whether the boles would yield the required size of planks and 'knees'. From a French treatise, 1710

150 *above*

The 50-gun Swedish warship AMARANTE (1653), showing her poop, quarterdeck and waist, and the detail of her rigging, construction and lavish decoration. This is the earliest surviving scale-model of a ship

151 *below*

Section of a three-decker of 1700. In the stern, the Captain's cabin is at the highest deck-level; the Admiral's cabin below it; the wardroom for lieutenants on the third deck below; the galley's flue is spouting smoke

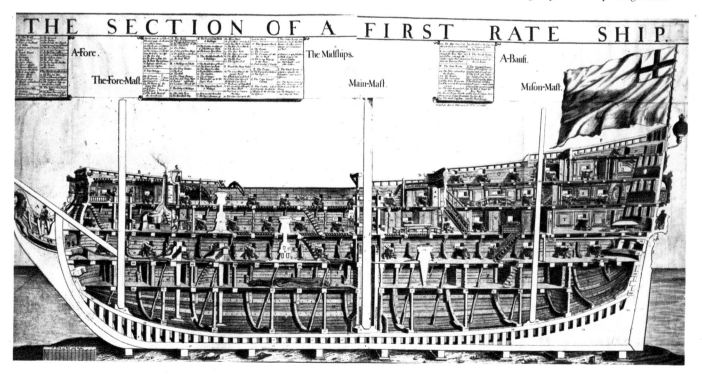

152
A detail from Van Keulen's *Atlas of the Waterworld* of 1682, showing buccaneers of Hispaniola with their navigational instruments — lead, compass, dividers, chart and cross-staff

The Brethren of the Coast

The complicated period of commercial, territorial and dynastic wars in Europe was enlivened by the exploits of freebooters in the Caribbean and the Pacific. Whatever treaties or alliances were concluded or broken in Europe, the custom of the day was 'no peace beyond the line'. The tropical seas swarmed with ruthless exponents of private enterprise who styled themselves pirates, buccaneers, slavers or privateers, as the mood took them. There was little to choose in the way of moral distinction between these titles, but the differences, though they were probably a little abstract in practice, are worth recording. A slaver was a merchant seaman engaged in a sad but then legal trade. A buccaneer, while not the lowest of the low, was nevertheless a raffish and rather suspect character, with the redeeming habit that he attacked all vulnerable shipping except that of his own country. Pirates attacked anyone they fancied, including each other, and were the enemies of mankind. A privateer was a merchant seaman or adventurer who held letters of marque. Granted by a competent authority, these letters defined the holders as belligerents, and entitled them to attack and capture vessels of countries hostile to their own, while exonerating them from any charge of piracy consequent upon such acts.

153 *left*

One of the early buccaneers, who were so called because they roasted meat in barbecues or *boucanes* (one of which is seen in the background) before they took to piracy at sea

154 *below*

Bartholomew the Portuguése, one of the earliest and cruellest of the buccaneers. His portrait comes from Esquemeling's *The Boucaniers of America*, a best-seller of its day

Pirates and Privateers

155 *left*
Sir Henry Morgan (1635-88), the greatest of the buccaneers of Jamaica. His capture of Panama in 1671 led the 'brethren of the coast' to the Pacific. Morgan himself died a respectable Deputy Governor of Jamaica

156 *above*
Bartering glass and cutlery for slaves and ivory in Guinea. From a Dutch chart of the Guinea coast between Gambia and Cape Verde

157 *left*
Captain Avery, known as 'Long Ben', led a mutiny in his ship and subsequently became a very successful pirate off the Guinea coast and in the Red Sea

158 *above*
Woodes Rogers, the English privateer, after he had returned with a hundred tons of gold from his voyage round the world, 1708-11. A painting by Hogarth, when Rogers was Governor of Bermuda and the scourge of pirates

159 *left*
The more usual ending to a pirate's life: a hanging at Execution Dock, Wapping, London, in the early eighteenth century

The earliest known illustration (Italian, seventeenth century) of King Neptune and his court baptising a 'subject' who is crossing the Equator for the first time

161 *below*
The first lighthouse to be built in England on the Eddystone rock near Plymouth. It was blown down in the great storm of 1703, killing its architect, Henry Winstanley

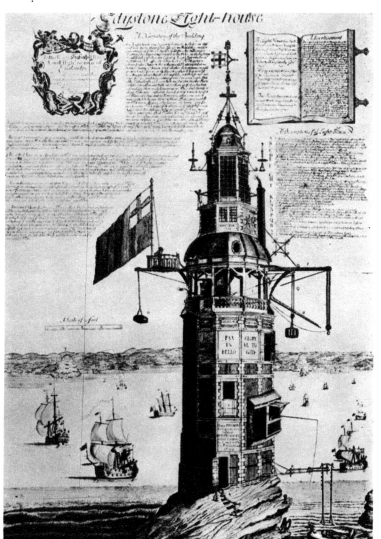

162
Frontispiece to the first edition of Defoe's *Robinson Crusoe*, based on the story of Alexander Selkirk, who was marooned on the island of Juan Fernandez by buccaneers. He lived there for three years until taken off by the English privateer, Woodes Rogers, in 1709

JEAN BART
Né à Dunkerque en 1650 Mort en 1702

Du grand Louis Jean Bart étendit la puissance
L'Empire de Thétis admira sa valeur
Et toujours ce soutien du pavillon de France
Sera de nos marins le modèle & l'honneur

163

Jean Bart (1650-1702), one of the heroes of
the French navy, who first made his reputation
by his privateering exploits in the North Sea.
Captured by the English, he made a daring
escape from Plymouth in a yawl, and returned
to ravage English shipping by lightning raids

CHAPTER VII
The World in Arms

The naval wars of the eighteenth century were all concerned with the struggle for a maritime empire. The first empire which Britain then won was based, as were all other empires at that time, on the assumptions of the old colonial system as laid down in the Navigation Acts, which were designed to enrich the mother country by canalising all trade to her ports and by encouraging merchant shipping by what we should now call 'flag discrimination'.

Sea-power has always depended on three factors — an efficient battle-fleet, a flourishing merchant marine from which men could be drawn for service in time of war, and overseas bases from which to launch land operations. By this date France and Britain had these three elements of sea-power; but it was the British who developed the strategy of maritime warfare by blockading the fleets of her enemies, so that combined operations for the conquest of colonial teritories could be safely undertaken from bases overseas. This strategy was carried out to perfection in the Seven Years War, when

164
A British frigate of the smallest, or 20 gun, class, on the stocks at Deptford, 1752. Painting by John Cleveley

165
The gorgeously carved stern of an early Georgian line-of-battle ship: a builder's model of the ROYAL WILLIAM, the longest-lived ship in the Royal Navy. She was launched in 1719 and remained in service till 1813

Britain seemed to have the prize of maritime empire within her grasp, but only thirteen years later the American Revolutionary War broke out, in which all the seagoing nations which she had previously defeated seized the opportunity for revenge. The consequence was the loss of her American colonies and the end of the old colonial system.

Warfare under sail was a highly skilled art. Not only were ships built for special purposes, either to lie in the line of battle or, as frigates, to act as cruisers and commerce destroyers, but tactics had become so formalised that a decisive battle became almost an impossibility. Between the Battle of Malaga in 1704 and the Battle of the Saints in 1782 no real victory was

166 *above*
Admiral Lord Anson, often called the Father of the Royal Navy on account of his reforms at the Admiralty, won fame by his circumnavigation of the world in 1740-44 in the 60-gun ship CENTURION, the first European warship to visit China. This portrait by Sir Joshua Reynolds shows him in the full-dress uniform of an admiral

167 *right*
The execution of Admiral Byng in 1757 on board his own quarter-deck. He was nominally shot for the loss of Minorca but, actually, according to Voltaire, '*pour encourager les autres.*' Marines formed the firing party, and the victim gave the signal by dropping his handkerchief

achieved in a formal sea battle. The decisive battles were those, as at Quiberon Bay, where tactics were in the nature of a 'general chase' and not those of the line-of-battle. The preservation of the close-hauled line-of-battle was regarded as sacrosanct, and the divisions of the line determined the naval hierarchy: the van, the centre, and the rear were commanded by a vice-admiral, fleet admiral and rear-admiral respectively. The English preferred offensive tactics, choosing the weather gauge in order to bear down and 'hull' the enemy, but the French countered this by firing high in order to immobilise them by damaging the masts and rigging. It was thus strategy rather than tactics which determined the outcome of a war.

168

Augustus Hervey (1725-86), Earl of Bristol, in the captain's uniform which he wore at the battle of Quiberon Bay in 1759. Portrait by Gainsborough

169 *left*
Admiral Boscawen (1711-61), nicknamed Wry-Necked Dick, by Reynolds. Pitt said to him, ' Others make difficulties, you find expedients. ' His victory at Lagos in 1759 helped to defeat the Spanish-French invasion threat

170 *right*
At the battle of Quiberon Bay in November 1759, Admiral Hawke defeated the French invasion threat. His flagship, the ROYAL GEORGE, is seen on the extreme right; the French flagship, SOLEIL ROYAL, which was wrecked, is seen on the left beyond the sinking THESEE in the foreground

171 *below*
The capture of Quebec in September 1759 was perhaps the most successful amphibious expedition ever undertaken, and an event of the greatest importance for the future of the American continent. General Wolfe's army is seen landing and fighting on the Plains of Abraham, while part of Admiral Saunders' fleet is on the right

172

A portrait of Admiral Sir Charles Saunders (1713-75) by Reynolds. He commanded the fleet which conveyed Wolfe to Quebec, and after his return, Pitt spoke of him as a man 'equalling those who have taken Armadas'. He subsequently became First Lord of the Admiralty

173 *above*
HMS WORCESTER under full sail. She was a 60-gun ship, and was present at the capture of Quebec. Drawing by Short

174 *below*
The stern of a model of the DAUPHIN ROYAL, a French 3-decker built in 1750

175
Launching a French 2-decker, the DUC DE BOURGOGNE, at Rochefort in 1751. For the occasion the ship was decorated with foliage

101

English Eighteenth-century Ships and Shipyards

176 *above*
A model of Deptford dockyard in 1770. The
large building on the left is the Victualling Yard.
In the centre, 'mast-ponds' and dry-docks,
and on the right stacks of seasoned timber

177 *below*
Launching a 3-decker at Deptford in 1757.
The large building is the Old Weevil, the
Victualling Yard. Painting by John Cleveley

178 *below*
Bow-view of a model of the ROYAL GEORGE.
Launched in 1757, she sank with all hands
in Portsmouth harbour in 1782 because her
timbers were rotten. She was the inspiration
of Cowper's poem, *Toll for the Brave*

179 *below*
Drawing of a 32-pounder gun from the ROYAL
GEORGE. These were the heaviest naval
guns of the time, firing a 32-pound solid shot
with a range of about 2,000 yards

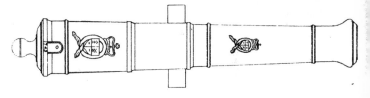

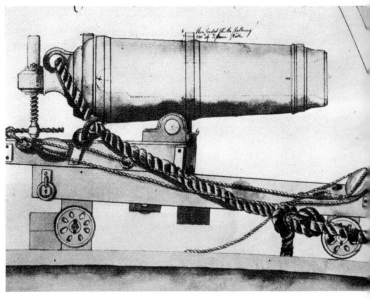

180 *right*
The carronade, like the modern mortar, was
a heavy short-range gun mounted on the upper
deck. Introduced in 1779, it became the vict-
ory-winning weapon in the days of Nelson

181

'A new mappe of a part of Hutson's or the North River.... surveyed in the Yare 1700 by Captain W. W. Römer', a German engineer. Part of Manhattan Island is at the top, with Staten Island in the centre, and New Jersey to the left

182 *below*

New York developed rapidly in the eighteenth century, particularly in the dock area. This plan of the city in 1776 shows its size at the outbreak of the War of Independence. New York was never attacked directly by sea

The American Revolutionary War

The events of the American war illustrate the naval strategy of the time. The new United States Navy was a puny force compared to the huge fleets of France and England, not to mention those of the Dutch and Spanish who also fought for their revenge. From the British point-of-view the war was lost when the command of the sea was lost and enemy fleets could sail across the ocean to the assistance of their ally. At the battle of the Chesapeake in 1781, the cause of American independence was really won because Washington appreciated the importance of sea-power by summoning the fleet of de Grasse to assist him in reducing the last British land-force at Yorktown. It was only because Rodney later won the battle of the Saints by disregarding formal tactics and breaking the French line that Canada and India were retained for Britain at the peace treaty.

Although the American colonists had no battle fleet, American shipping had greatly increased, so that the American effort at sea was chiefly in the guise of privateering. John Paul Jones, though a commissioned officer, was really a privateer of genius. Apart from the damage done to English commerce by this means, the French navy at this time was at the peak of its efficiency, as the British had been in the preceding war. After this period of adversity the Royal Navy was to rise again in the age of Nelson.

183
' Black Dick ' Howe, the British Admiral commanding the North American Station in the early years of the War of Independence, when his brother commanded the army on land. Known as ' the sailor's friend ' because of the care he took of his men, his most famous victory was at the Glorious First of June in the Bay of Biscay in 1794. Portrait by Copley

184 *below*
New York in 1760, when it was still a British colony. A British frigate lies off-shore

185 *above*, and 186 *right*
Two portraits of John Paul Jones. To the left, an English representation of this famous raider of their coasts in the guise of a pirate, with his ship in flames. To the right, a heroic bust by the French sculptor Houdon done after Jones' retirement to France, where he died in poverty in 1790

187 *above*
The action fought off Flamborough Head on 23 September 1779, between Jones' two privateers and Captain Pearson's frigate HMS SERAPIS, which is seen in the left foreground, with Jones' BONHOMME RICHARD behind her and her consort to the right. Having told Pearson, who called on him to surrender, 'I have not yet begun to fight', Jones boarded and acptured the English frigate just before his own ship sank under him. Engraving after R. Paton

The Battle of the Chesapeake

188 *right*, and 189 *below*

Two views (never previously reproduced) of the battle in the Chesapeake on 5 September, 1781, when a French fleet under de Grasse assisted Washington to force the last British army to surrender at Yorktown. The upper drawing shows the French (left) coming out of harbour and the British (right) approaching in line ahead at 1.0 pm. The lower drawing shows the situation at 3.45 pm. when Graves (right) has worn before the wind and is attacking with his van. The rest of his fleet never came into action, so that de Grasse escaped unscathed. Note that the big ships lie in the line, the frigates keeping out of the battle

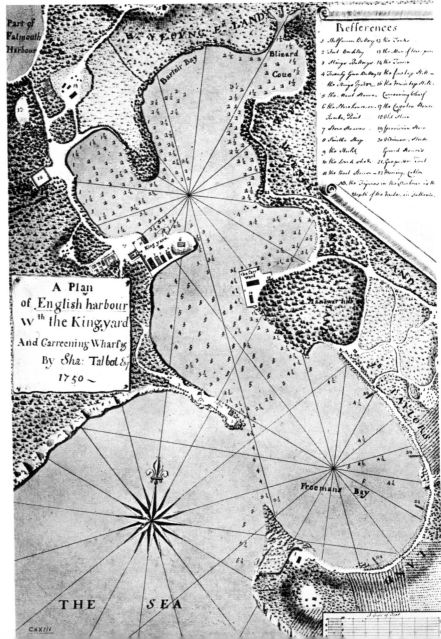

190 *above*
Admiral Sir Hyde Parker (1714-82), by Romney. He was second-in-command in the West Indies during the American war. This shows the uniform of an admiral before stripes were added to his sleeves

191 *above, right*
Caricature of Lord Rodney receiving the surrender of de Grasse after the battle of the Saints in the West Indies on 12 April 1782, a naval victory which enabled Britain to retain Canada and India, though the United States had already won her freedom

192 *right*
Chart of English Harbour, Antigua, one of the principal British bases at that time, and so frequently used by the young Captain Nelson that it is often called Nelson's Harbour. It has recently been restored to its original condition

A Dus vertoond hem de Moordenaars Baij als gy op 15 vademen daar in geankert Zijt

New Dominions

After the loss of the American colonies, Britain turned to develop a trading empire in India, and then, after the discovery of Australia and New Zealand, to found new colonies in the Pacific. The first task was left in the main to private enterprise in the form of the East India Company, which, founded nearly two hundred years before, was now so large and powerful that it had armies and fleets of its own. The second was the result of government-sponsored voyages of exploration.

The story of the discovery of Australia originates in the ancient belief that a great southern continent lay in the Pacific and Atlantic. The first attempt to define its extent was made by Abel Tasman in 1642 at the order of Van Diemen, the governor of the Dutch East India Company in Java. The western coast had already been found; so had the northern in 1606; but how far south did the continent extend? Tasman discovered the island

193 *above*

Abel Tasman discovered the west coast of New Zealand in 1642, when he was sent by the Dutch East India Company to discover the extent of Australia. He found Tasmania, and then sailed east to the coast of New Zealand, which he named, but the Maoris seen in the picture drove him off the west coast

194
Louis Antoine de Bougainville, Cook's predecessor in the Pacific, who was prevented from discovering the east coast of Australia in 1768 when he was nearly wrecked on the Great Barrier Reef

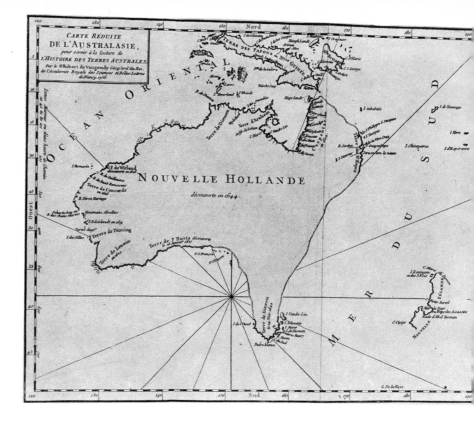

195 right
Map of New Holland (Australia) before the
voyage of Captain Cook, who took with him
this map made in France in 1756. The map
confused the New Hebrides islands with the
north-east coast, and no eastern coast of New
Zealand was known before Cook's voyage

196 below
Newcastle-on-Tyne in 1724, where young James
Cook first went to sea in colliers, and learned
to be the greatest sailor of his age

197 *left*
Portrait of James Cook (1728-79) by Nathaniel Dance, painted after his second voyage of 1772-5, when he had been promoted Captain

198 *below*
Sir Joseph Banks (1743-1820), who accompanied Cook on his first voyage, and later promoted the first settlement of Australia. He is here shown by the painter Benjamin West wearing Maori costume

which bears his name, and also the west coast of New Zealand. But he did not find the eastern coasts either of New Holland (Australia) or New Zealand. So when, a century later, the explorers of the age of Cook took up the search, the map of those parts was still extraordinarily incomplete and inaccurate.

From 1764 onwards a series of French and English explorers raced each other round the globe to discover what appeared to be the last remaining prize of empire. Of these Captain Cook was preeminent, the finest seaman Britain ever produced. In his three voyages between 1768 and his death in Hawaii in 1779, he finally demolished the myth of the southern continent, replacing it with the reality of Australia, New Zealand, as well as discovering the north-west coast of America. Two of his companions have earned their niche in history: Captain Bligh, whose crew mutinied in the *Bounty*; and George Vancouver, who carefully retraced his route along the western coast of Canada.

The modern map of the Pacific is Cook's memorial; but we must not forget his two other achievements — the improvement of health at sea, and the determination of longitude. Both were problems of long standing and of

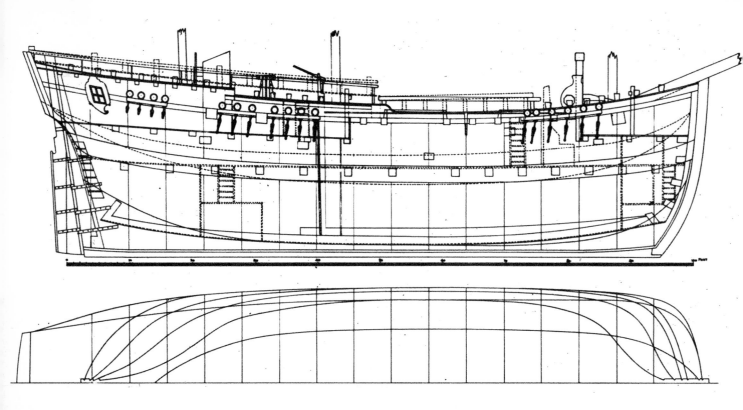

the utmost importance. Ten times the number of seamen were lost by unsuitable food and poor conditions of hygiene than were killed in action or lost in shipwreck. What Cook did was to demonstrate the rightness of other men's ideas, such as Dr James Lind's cure of scurvy by lemon-juice (though Cook himself had preferred other specifics, such as sauerkraut and portable or preserved soup). A few years later French scientists produced canned meat, so that the next generation of explorers could for the first time preserve their food. Equally important in the story of man's conquest of the sea was the determination of longitude, so that a ship's captain could at last find out where he was by means of the chronometer. Cook's last two voyages demonstrated the accuracy of Harrison's timekeeper, which thenceforward became a standard part of a ship's equipment. Cook was now able to set a new standard in cartography, and sailors could safely sail ' by God and the Admiralty chart. '

201 *below*

The Mutiny of the BOUNTY, after leaving
the island of Tahiti in 1789. Captain Bligh is
being turned away in the longboat at the
start of his 3,000 mile voyage to Timor.
Fletcher Christian, the ring-leader of the muti-
neers, is seen between the breadfruit trees
which Bligh was to have carried to the West
Indies. Aquatint by R. Dodd

The Problem of Distance

202 *left*
Cook's RESOLUTION (left) and ADVEN-
TURE (right) at Tahiti, on his second voyage
in 1773. Painted by the artist who accompanied him, William Hodges

203 *below*
The RESOLUTION in the Antarctic in 1773.
A boat's crew breaks up an ice-floe for water,
while an officer shoots down an albatross.
Drawing by Hodges

204
Harrison's fourth model of the chronometer, constructed by Larcum Kendal, which proved the answer to the age-old problem of finding longitude. Cook used it on his second voyage

205
John Harrison (1693-1776), the inventor of the chronometer, with his fourth model or watch on the table beside him, and his first larger model behind him

Mulgrave

July 1775
Sat: 22ᵈ When after two hours calm, in the Latitude of 39..38 S° we got the Wind at West, the next day it had at N.N.W. and increased to a fresh gale, with which we steered directly for the Lizard and on

Sat: 29ᵗʰ We made the Land about Plymouth. Maker Church, at 5 o'clock in the After-noon, bore N.10.W. distant 4 leagues: this bearing and distance, shew'd that the error of Mʳ Kendals Watch, in Longitude was only 7'.45; which was too far to the West —

Jam⁵ Cook

206
The concluding sentence of Cook's journal in 1775, observing that 'the error of Mr Kendal's watch in Longitude was only 7' 45'', which was too far to the West', that is, the watch was a trifle slow after three years at sea in every sort of temperature and weather

207
A naval captain. Lord George Graham, painted by Hogarth in 1745, dines in his cabin attended by his cook, his purser, and a one-man band. The Captain's dog wears his master's wig, and the cook pours gravy down the chaplain's neck

CHAPTER VIII   **The Seaman's Life**

Dr Johnson said that life on board ship was worse than life in gaol, with the additional danger of drowning. His opinion was certainly shared by his humbler contemporaries, and the Navy was unpopular enough to be permanently short of able-bodied men. There was always a hard core of prime seamen in the fleet, and it received a steady stream of volunteers attracted by promises of lavish bounties and prize-money in time of war; but there were never enough to make up the total of 130,000 men required to man the six hundred ships in commission in Nelson's day, and when the fleet put to sea, the crews were largely composed of merchant sailors, pressed men and gaolbirds.

The press-gangs were often brutal in their methods, and, as the cartoons and romances of the time make clear, they caused great suffering to the families left behind and sometimes acted beyond the broad limits permitted them by a law that did not err on the side of sentiment. But in times of crisis, the need for men was desperate, so desperate that men were often impressed out of ships at sea, even out of foreign ships, and it was this odious practice which led to the only war fought between Great Britain and the United States, once the latter had won her freedom. It should not be forgotten, however, that a large number of deserters were recovered in this way, and that once

208
The press gang in action on Tower Hill towards the end of the eighteenth century. The lieutenant in charge is on the right; the toughest member of his gang is in the centre

209 *below*
A midshipmen's mess of 1821. As ever, music, cards, wine and practical jokes pass the time, against a background of sextants, dirks, and speaking trumpets

210
A cartoon by Gillray, ironically entitled 'The
Liberty of the Subject', depicts another aspect
of the press-gang, which was the normal
method of manning the Fleet in the eighteenth century

aboard, a tough, jovial camaraderie developed between the sailors that did
much to compensate for the harsh life they led.

When a ship was commissioned, her sailors were rounded up and sent aboard,
where they were quartered into divisions, gun-crews and messes. Until 1857,
the British sailor did not possess a uniform: he went barefoot, dressed in
purser's slops, that is, any old clothes that were available on board, and he
made a habit of wearing his hat clamped to the back of his head. He
ate 'salt horse' and weevily biscuits off tables slung from deck-beams that
stood rather less than six feet above the deck-boards on which he lived.
He drank his rum, neat until Admiral Vernon introduced 'grog' by
diluting it with water. He slept in a hammock which was rolled up and
stowed away when not in use; and he normally chewed tobacco, as it was
forbidden to smoke a pipe except in the galley. He was required to
attend Sunday service and the punishment of his mates. He took his
women where he could find them (and women were allowed on board
when the ship was in port), and the discipline under which he lived
was strict and harshly enforced. He used muttonfat for sunburn, anything
he could lay his hands on to keep out the cold, and when it came to a crisis,
he could fight like a demon. If he survived his diet, his battles, his punish-
ments, his loves and the elements, he could retire as a pensioner to Greenwich Hospital (a magnificent setting for the last years of men so brutalised
during their service), and boast until the end of his days that the young
naval recruits did not know what hardship was.

211 *above*
Another cartoonist, Samuel Rowlandson, illustrates the horrors of the press-gang

212 *left*
All hands are turned out to witness the flogging of a seaman, while marines stand guard on the fo'c'stle. The midshipmen and officers are grouped in the foreground. Cruikshank is here illustrating a story in which the real offender stands forth to save a shipmate from unjust punishment at the gratings

213 *right*

In 1782 Rowlandson went down to Portsmouth to make pictures of the recently sunk ROYAL GEORGE. In this drawing he gives his impression of the Middle Deck of the line-of-battle ship HECTOR. Women were allowed on board when the ship was in port

Above and below Decks

214 *below*

The morning watch 'holystoning' the quarter-deck under the eye of a lieutenant. The term 'holy' was attached to the oblong blocks of pumice-stone because they resembled bibles. Sketch by Captain Marryat

215 *below*
Social intercourse between decks aboard a warship in port, about 1799. The bulging cocoons hanging from the deckhead are sailors' hammocks

215 *below*
Social intercourse between decks aboard a warship in port, about 1799. The bulging cocoons hanging from the deckhead are sailors' hammocks

Naval Officers

Unlike the practice in the army, naval commissions could not be bought. Serving officers came mostly from families with a naval tradition, or with relatives in the service, and promotion depended as much on influential family connections as on the fortunes of war. Politics also played a large part in the acquisition of commands, but since senior naval officers were apt to find themselves in the position of ambassadors, governors and representatives of the Crown in distant places at difficult times, the system was not without its advantages. Except in the case of a Master, who navigated the ship, there was little promotion from the lower deck, and a good deal of friction occurred between such officers as came up from there and the gentleman captains. Samuel Pepys had partly solved this problem in the previous century, for gentlemen and seamen alike, by setting a lieutenants' examination as a hurdle to commissioned rank. Like most examinations, it had unexpected results, and a midshipman in his 'teens often found himself in the company of a greybeard of equal rank who had failed his exams.

216 *above*
An unknown lieutenant dressed in the new uniform of 1748. Portrait by Reynolds

217 *below*
Captain Bentinck (who invented the chain-pump) encourages in his son a love of ships and the sea. Painting by Chamberlain, 1775

218 *above*
A sketch by Rowlandson of a midshipman

219 *above, right*
A Rowlandson caricature of Admiral Paisley

220 *below, left*
Midshipmen were never flogged, but they were frequently 'mast-headed' by the first lieutenant, as this drawing by Rowlandson shows

221 *below*
William IV in the uniform of a midshipman of 1780. He became the last naval officer to bear the title Lord High Admiral of England

222 *above*
A sailor heaving the lead, about 1807

223 *above*
One-legged sea-cook, by Rowlandson

224 *below*
A boy-sailor with a soup-bowl, by Rowlandson

225 *below*
The purser, or supply-officer, by Rowlandson

Naval Types

226 *left*

Quarter-deck of the DEAL CASTLE, during a voyage home from the West Indies in 1775. Awnings give shade to the Captain's livestock and the man at the wheel. A midshipman ascends the gangway from the waist. Water-colour by Thomas Hearne

227 *below*

Sailors relax in the waist of a ship in port. The card-player on the right is sitting on a box of 24 lb grape-shot, while the fiddler sits on a rack of solid round-shot. The spar deck overhead is so named because it carries the spare spars

228
Figurehead of HMS CENTURION, 1844

229
Figurehead of HMS BELLEROPHON, 1818

230 *right*
Rowlandson's panorama of Portsmouth Point about 1790. The shop on the left is a money-lender's, and the one on the right a tavern patronised by officers, which still exists. Seamen, much the worse for liquor, litter the quayside

Officers and Men

231 *below*
The Master and his mate present 'the young gentlemen' with a problem in navigation, while the cabin lists heavily. An illustration by Peacock for Falconer's poem *The Shipwreck*

232 *above*
Going aboard the HECTOR. A sketch by
Rowlandson in Portsmouth harbour of a typ-
ical 2-decker of seventy-four guns

233 *below*
The lieutenants' wardroom of HMS GLOUCES-
TER in 1812, sketched by the ship's chaplain. The stern window is beyond the end
of the table, and the doors and partitions on
either side were stowed when the ship was
cleared for action

The East India Company

Less than two centuries after its formation by a group of Elizabethan merchant adventurers, the East India Company had become, in effect, the government of India, having its own army, its own navy, its own flag, and a fleet of merchantmen which were probably the best found and certainly the biggest ships then afloat. These early freighters on the Far East run were not owned outright by the Company, but were chartered from private ownership and entrusted to captains who were permitted to trade on their own account as well as in the Company's interests. The service was as honourable as it was lucrative, and many captains were enabled to buy their own ships, and charter them to the Company. These vessels varied in size from 500 to 1,400 tons, and by the end of the eighteenth century there were over a hundred ships in the Company's service. In its own waters, the Company enjoyed a large measure of political autonomy, but its ships were not allowed to fly the Company flag north of St Helena, and in home waters their crews frequently met with the same fate that so enraged the Americans: the Royal Navy took their best sailors. The losses were so serious that the Company began to ship a proportion of Lascars and Goanese in their crews.

235 *above*
Bombay in the early eighteenth century with
Indiamen in the foreground

236 *below*
Canton, in 1805, the centre of eastern trade
with the western world. Along the waterfront,
from right to left, are the 'factories' of the
Dutch, English and Danish merchant companies

East Indian Pride

237 *right,* **238** *below*

A builder's model of the Dutch East India-man DER ARY, built in 1725 when decorated sterns were still in fashion. The mizzen mast is lateen-rigged, the others square-rigged. The deck view shows the waist of the ship, which, as usual, was heavily armed. The poop, half-deck and quarter-deck are clearly distinguishable. Here the officers and passengers lived, the crew having their quarters before the main mast

239 *left*
The earliest surviving example of a compass
card floating on a needle in a bowl. It was
made in England in 1750

240 *below*
Launching of an East Indiaman at Blackwall
in 1827. Such ships averaged 1,200 tons, and
though they were normally heavily armed,
one tier of gun-ports were often dummies
to give the appearance of a warship

Trade with the Orient

241
Officers of the East India Company in 1840, shortly before its end. One of the officers holds a speaking trumpet

242 *left*
A Japanese artist's impression of the Dutch East Indiaman SHELLACK, bringing cloth, spices and aromatic woods to Nagasaki in 1782. The Dutch obtained permission to trade with the Japanese, but for many years the privilege was confined to one ship a year

243
The EARL BALCARRES, an East Indiaman
of 1,488 tons launched at Bombay in 1815
and constructed of teak, then first coming
into fashion as a building material. These
ships were more flush-decked than warships.
The lower row of gun-ports were dummies

Calm and Storm

244 *left*
Sir Stanford Raffles (1781-1826), who obtained for the East India Company the uninhabited island that became Singapore in 1819. Raffles was Governor of Java and the founder of the London Zoo

246 *opposite, above*
A humorous drawing by George Cruikshank of the great cabin of an Indiaman in a gale. This was the passengers' cabin, and their wine was slung from the rafters on cords to prevent spilling. The drawing is dated 1815

247 *opposite, below*
A painting by an unknown artist of the English Indiaman HALSEWELL, about 1800. The picture is entitled 'Society at sea'

245 *below*
The captain's table aboard the East Indiaman CLYDE in a heavy swell. The Army officer to the right appears to have little relish for the next course

248

Horatio Nelson (1758-1805). This portrait, by Rigaud, was begun when Nelson was a lieutenant aged 19, and was not completed until two years later, by which time he had already been promoted Captain

250 *below*

Tom Allen, Nelson's bo'sun, who fought at Trafalgar and ended his days as a pensioner at Greenwich Hospital

249

Admiral Duncan at the battle of Camperdown which was fought against the Dutch in 1797

CHAPTER IX
The Navies of Nelson and America

If war is an art, as strategists claim it to be, and if methods of destruction can attain to a classical form, as some historians affirm, then the classical period of warfare at sea under sail opened roughly about 1792 and ended in 1815. Thirty-seven years later the first battleship designed for steam, the *Agamemnon*, was built, and by the middle of the century sailing navies had vanished from the sea.

The French Revolutionary Wars and the Napoleonic campaigns came at a fortunate moment in England's history, hard on the heels of naval and medical reforms and the upsurge of vitality that sprang from them. Her Navy was in good shape. Developments in many fields, such as gunnery, signals and ship construction, had greatly increased its fighting efficiency, and she had men: Nelson, Collingwood, Cornwallis, Hood, the ageing but implacable Howe, Jervis, Duncan, Exmouth, Cochrane and many others.

251
Lieutenant Pellew, son of Lord Exmouth,
leading a boarding party off Java in 1812

252
Lord Cochrane, Earl of Dundonald, the greatest frigate captain of the age, later known
for his part in winning the independence of
Chile, Peru, Brazil and Greece

253 *below*
Lord St Vincent (1735-1823) won the battle
of Cape St Vincent in 1797, and trained the
fleets which Nelson led to victory. Portrait
by Stuart painted in 1783

Unfortunately for France her navy was at its lowest ebb. Not that her
sailors lacked in courage; on the contrary, they fought gallantly. But the
revolutionaries, the slaves of their own doctrines, had exiled or executed
so many senior officers that there were not enough to go round when war
was declared, and the French were obliged to make admirals from lieutenants,
which put an unfair strain on everyone but the enemy.

In spite of these advantages, England opened the war in a fumbling fashion,
her gross errors of strategy being redeemed from time to time by resounding
victories, such as Howe's defeat of Villaret-Joyeuse, on 1 June 1794. Three
years later naval mutinies at Spithead and the Nore paralysed the fleet for
several months, but in the same year Duncan defeated the Dutch at Camperdown, and at Cape St Vincent Sir John Jervis (later Lord St Vincent)
defeated the hapless Spaniards, who had reluctantly entered the war on the
French side. It was during the battle of St Vincent that Nelson undertook
a highly successful independent manoeuvre which added lustre to the victory
and brought public renown to his name for the first time. Before then, his
qualities had undoubtedly been noticed, but only in the Navy.

254 *above*

Nelson, severely wounded in the head at the Battle of the Nile (1798) has the wound dressed in the cockpit of the VANGUARD. The seaman whose leg is about to be amputated would probably be drugged with wine or opium. Aquatint by M. Dubourg after Heath

The next eight years were all his, and he marked them indelibly as his **own** with three brilliant victories: the battle of the Nile (1798), Copenhagen (1801) and Trafalgar (1805). It is interesting to note that the original draft of his Trafalgar signal was 'Nelson expects...', and that it was his devoted yeoman of signals who persuaded him to change it to the text which has become immortal: 'England expects that every man will do his duty'. After Nelson's death, war continued for a further ten years. During this time, the by now unchallenged mistress of the seas strangled the acknowledged master of the Continent with her blockading fleets, while she annexed at the same time his colonies and those of his unwilling allies, Spain and Holland. At the end of hostilities, England had defeated Europe and gained the Cape of Good Hope, Ceylon, Malta and a string of other useful possessions. For the next ninety-nine years the Empire basked in the wartmh and security of the Pax Britannica, a peace which reposed on supreme sea-power.

255 below
The Battle of the Nile, when Nelson destroyed Napoleon's fleet in Aboukir Bay. The action is viewed from the rear of the French line at anchor, with the British ships beginning to envelop their van. Six frigates are moored on the left

New Methods of War

256 above, 257 right
A revolutionary weapon invented at this date was Congreve's incendiary rocket, with a warhead of 32 lbs and an extreme range of 3,000 yards. They were first fired from small boats under the command of Sir Home Popham (above), against Napoleon's invasion barges at Boulogne in 1804

258 *above*
Nelson's victory over the Danish fleet in Copenhagen, in 1801. The Danish fleet at anchor before the town was attacked by Nelson with the shallower draft ships of the British fleet under Sir Hyde Parker

259 *left*
One of the many plans for the invasion of England, showing the flotillas of barges which were to carry Napoleon's Grand Army of 56,000 men across the Channel from Boulogne

Trafalgar

260 *right*
A drawing by the Spanish Chief-of-staff showing the British fleet attacking the Franco-Spanish fleet in a loose crescent formation off Cape Trafalgar on 21 October 1805. Collingwood's column is in action to the left; Nelson's VICTORY leads the column on the right to cut the enemy's line

261 *below*
The death of Nelson on the quarterdeck of the VICTORY at Trafalgar, with midshipman Pollard aiming at the marksman who shot him from the tops of the French ship RE-DOUBTABLE. The officer with his back turned is Captain Hardy. Painting by D. Deighton, done shortly after the war was over

262

The VICTORY, her mizzen, foretopmast and wheel shot away, was towed towards the shelter of Gibraltar harbour after the battle. Twenty of the enemy's thirty-three ships were taken or sunk at Trafalgar; not one of the British fleet of twenty-seven was lost. The VICTORY'S flag flies at half-mast for the death of Nelson

Wooden Walls

The ships of Nelson's day were rated as follows:

1st-rate	. . .	Three-deckers	. . . . . .	100 guns and over
2nd-rate	. . .	Three-deckers	. . . . . .	90 guns and over
3rd-rate	. . .	Two-deckers	. . . .	74 guns and over
4th-rate	. . .	Two-deckers	. . . . . .	50 guns and over
5th-rate	. . .	Single-decker frigates	. . .	32 guns and over
6th-rate	. . .	Single-decker frigates	. . .	24 guns and over

The first four rates were the line-of-battle ships. The frigates were the destroyers of the age, light, fast, and in talented hands (notably under American frigate captains) they carried a considerable punch. The sloops, schooners and brigs were employed in convoy, escort and despatch work. Towards the end of the century there was a marked improvement in the condition of hulls owing to the introduction of copper sheathing below the waterline, and at the same time the Admiralty took to spending money in more functional ways, probably because there was less of it to spend. The gorgeous gilded ornamentation of ships was already out of fashion, the whipstaff and tiller had long been replaced by the wheel, and the ships' topsides were painted in broad strakes of black, yellow or white. The inside was painted uniformly red (to save repainting after a battle). Royals and studding sails were now in general use, the spritsail had vanished, and the old mizzen yard had been replaced by a spanker gaff. The sole surviving example of a first-rate line-of-battle ship is Nelson's *Victory*, which still flies the flag of the Commander-in-chief at Portsmouth.

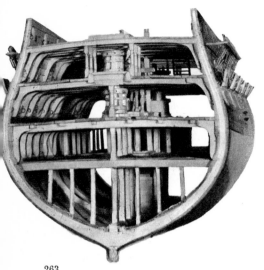

263
The backbone of the Navy — the 74-gun third-rate, shown in a 1795 sectional model. Note the inner and outer planking of the hull, the two gun-decks with capstans above the waterline and the orlop deck below

264 *below*
The bows of HMS VICTORY, showing the figurehead below the bowsprit and the anchor ' catted ' in the chains. A view taken in the dry-dock at Portsmouth where she lies today

265 *below, right*
HMS VICTORY floodlit at Portsmouth. The gangway and entry port are seen aft, the admiral's cabin in the stern

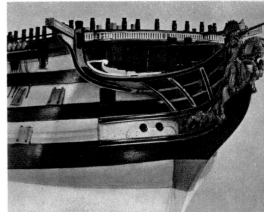

266 *left*

The US frigate CONSTITUTION, nicknamed 'Old Ironsides', which defeated the JAVA and other English frigates in the War of 1812-14. Built at Boston in 1797, she is the only surviving frigate of the period. She was 1,576 tons and carried 44 guns

267 *above*

One of the last of the detailed builder's models: the bows of the BOYNE (1790), St Vincent's flagship. The figurehead represents William III at the battle of the Boyne

268 *below*

A sectional drawing of the VICTORY. She was a 3-decker — three gun decks, and the orlop below the water-line. The living quarters in the stern (reading downwards from the top deck) were the captain's cabin, the admiral's cabin and the ward-room. Nelson died in the cockpit marked A

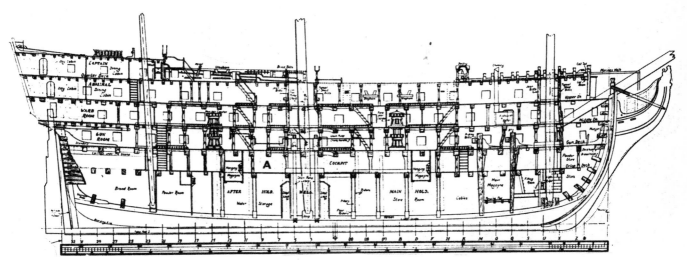

269 *opposite* and 270 *below*
A detailed and general view of a bone model
of the 2,500 ton 3-decker OCEAN, made by
French prisoners-of-war from memory while
in British captivity. She was the French
flagship which Nelson sank at the battle of
the Nile in 1798. The rigging of the model,
which is in the Science Museum, London, was
made of human hair

Conflict between French and English

271
The French frigate LA POMONE painted by
Roux in 1797. Under full sail, she was reputed
the fastest frigate afloat. When the British
captured her, they used her lines in the building of new ships

272 *above*
An English ship towing a French privateer, which captured her in the Channel in 1797. The British flag has been reversed to show that she is a captured prize. Drawing by Ozanne

273 *below*
A typical frigate, HMS AMETHYST (36 guns), in chase of the French THETIS (40 guns) in 1808. Such single-decked frigates, serving as convoy escorts, fulfilled many of the roles now undertaken by destroyers

Anglo-American War (1812-1814)

The closing years of the struggle in Europe were bedevilled by a deplorable outbreak of war between England and America. It arose from the clash between two irreconcilable policies: the neutral's everlasting cry of 'Freedom of the Seas', and the blunt retort of 'Belligerent's Rights', which must come from any nation engaged in war. England insisted on her right to impress British nationals out of foreign ships, and her right to search neutral vessels for contraband. The United States resisted, and war was declared by Congress on 18 June 1812. Hostilities were much enlivened by a series of single-ship actions, most of which the Americans won, and their jubilation at the success of these dashing encounters obscured the solemn fact that their coasts were blockaded throughout, virtually without opposition. At

274 *above*
Sir George Cockburn, Commander-in-chief of the British fleet in American waters in 1814. The city burning behind him is Washington

275 *right*
Captain Broke of the English frigate SHANNON (52 guns) leading a boarding party to the capture of the US frigate CHESAPEAKE (50 guns) off Boston on 1 June 1813. Lawrence, Captain of the CHESAPEAKE, was killed exclaiming, 'Don't give up the ship'. More men were killed during this fifteen-minute action than were lost at the battle of St Vincent

276 *above*
Captain Decatur's UNITED STATES frigate of 54 guns, often called 'Old Waggoner'. She has dismasted the British frigate MACEDO-NIAN of 49 guns off the Canary Islands, on 25 October 1812

the outset, Britain's naval and military forces were fully absorbed in her struggle with Napoleon, and little was done to reinforce British garrisons and naval squadrons in the American theatre. After Napoleon's fall Britain was able to send troops to America. The American armies, having fumbled the start of the inland campaigns, now began to fight far more effectively in the face of much greater opposition. Naval and military engagements in this short war occurred over an enormous area: from the Great Lakes to New Orleans, from Valparaiso to the Brazilian coast and the mouth of the English Channel. The absurdity of the war soon became apparent to both participants. American trade was going to ruin, and England — exhausted by decades of continuous warfare — wanted peace. A treaty was signed on Christmas Eve 1814 in Ghent; but owing to the slow communications of the period, isolated battles continued for several months, and the final action was not fought until 23 March 1815.

277 below
Captain Perry, commanding the American flotilla on Lake Erie in the 1812 war, defeated the British off Detroit. Captain Perry is being pulled across to receive the surrender of a British brig

278 *left*
The American frigate ESSEX, the first American warship in the Pacific, was captured by HMS PHOEBE off Valparaiso in 1813. She was 867 tons, and mounted 46 guns

279 *below*
During the war between the United States and Tripoli in 1803, Captain Bainbridge's PHILADELPHIA was captured, but Lieutenant Decatur set her alight in harbour before rowing away. Nelson, then blockading Toulon, called it 'the most daring act of the age'

CHAPTER X
The Golden Age of Sail

280 *left*
Ship's figurehead, carved by Samuel McIntyre of Salem, 1800

281 *below*
The East Indiaman HEREFORDSHIRE, built at Bombay of teak in 1813. She was 1,342 tons, and was armed with 26 guns. Painting by Huggins

During the lengthy passage of a dozen centuries or more the sailing ship
in all her stages met the changing needs of trade and war, and then, within
the span of a man's life, she found her finest form in the clipper ship and
vanished from the seas. It is just ninety years since the *Cutty Sark*
was built and launched for the China tea trade: today she lies in dry dock
at Greenwich, a stately memorial to the great days of sail which came to an
end some sixty years ago. Historically, the clipper epoch is still on the horizon
of our times; technologically, those pyramids of canvas are several worlds
away from turbo-jets and nuclear power. Yet there is something about the
clipper ships that cannot be forgotten, and there is today as much contro-
versy as ever over their finer points, their best day's run, and the vexed question: Who built the first clipper hull? Some claim the honour for the 500-
ton schooner *Ann McKimm* of Baltimore (1832); others favour the 142-ton
schooner *Scottish Maid*, built by Hall's of Aberdeen in 1839; but according to present opinion, which is not universally accepted, the first clipper
ship — clipper hull, ship rigged — was the *Rainbow* of 750 tons, launched
at New York in 1845.

The term 'clipper', by itself, did not refer to any special rig or any partic-
ular size of hull; it described a completely new way of building a ship's
bows, knife-sharp at the waterline, flared above it, the 'lines of entrance'
concave. The long clipper bows cut rather than pushed their way through
the water, unlike the convex apple-cheeked bows of earlier hulls. Whoever
was the inventor, there is no doubt that the Americans took the lead after

282
The clipper MARCO POLO. In 1855 she
claimed that she logged 470 miles in twenty-
four hours. Built as a Quebec timber ship, she
was converted into an emigrant clipper, and
made a record passage from England to Melbourne in sixty-eight days

1845 in developing the idea, and up until the Civil War they produced some of the finest of the great clippers ever launched. Of these, the best came from the shipyards of Donald McKay. He made his name with the *Flying Cloud* in 1850. His *Great Republic* was the largest wooden ship ever built, and on the San Francisco run she logged 413 miles in twenty-four hours. The four big clippers, all over 2,000 tons, which he sold to Baines of Liverpool, were the fastest that ever sailed the seas. They were: *Lightning*, 436 miles in twenty-four hours; *Champion of the Seas*, 465 miles in twenty-four hours; the *Donald McKay*, and the *James Baines*, the latter once attaining the speed of twenty-one knots.

The emigrant trade from Europe to the New World, and the discovery of gold in America and Australia, gave a tremendous impetus to the ship-building trade. During the first year of the Californian gold-rush, 90,000 passengers were carried round the Horn to San Francisco and in the boom years of the Australian gold-fields, British clippers carried 400,000 passengers to and from the colony. Emigrant ships crossed the Atlantic in fourteen

283 *above*
The British clipper MALABAR (1,350 tons), built for Green's Blackwall line in 1860. She made the Calcutta-Dover passage in eighty-nine days

284 *right*
The last surviving clipper, the CUTTY SARK, now preserved in dry-dock at Greenwich, England. Built at Dumbarton in 1869, she was of 963 tons, 212 feet in length and 36 feet beam. Designed for the China trade, she later proved to be one of the fastest emigrant ships on the Australian run. Her curious name, which means Ragged Skirt, was taken from an incident in Burns' *Tam O'Shanter*

285
ARIEL (left) and TAEPING, two of three racing tea-clippers which left Foo Chow on 30 May 1866. They quickly lost touch, and did not sight each other until the end of the voyage ninety-nine days later, when they docked on the same tide after a close race up the English Channel. They are here shown passing the Lizard

days. London to Melbourne could be made in sixty-four days, and Mc-Kay's *Flying Cloud* sailed from New York to San Francisco in ninety-eight days via Cape Horn. Coincident with the outbreak of the American Civil War, there was a slump in world freight rates, and American ship-building declined. At the same time the 'composite hull' arrived (iron frame, wood planking), and then the iron-hulled steamship. The *Cutty Sark* is an example of the composite hull, and it was with such ships that the British shipowners drove their American competitors from the eastern seas.

286 *above*
The owner's wife, perhaps?

287 *above*
A mermaid on the bows
of an American clipper

288 *right*
Figurehead of the American clipper
GEORGE R. SKOLFIELD

289 *above* and 290 *above right*
The Californian gold-rush diverted much Atlantic traffic to the Pacific via the Horn or the Panama overland route. The ENTERPRIZE took the Panama route. The DAVID CROCKETT, a clipper of 1,679 tons, made a record passage to San Francisco via the Horn in 103 days

291 *below*
South Street, in New York, in 1880. The vessel on the left is the Swallowtail packet LEEDS

Ships for Emigrants

292

Irish emigrants on their way to the New World in 1850. They are seen waiting on the quay at Cork, ready to embark

293

Paddle-steamers were used on the emigrant routes as well as clipperships. These two, NIMROD and ATHLONE, are leaving Dublin for Liverpool in 1851, which was the chief port of departure

294

The best-accredited account of a sea-serpent comes from the crew of HMS DAEDALUS. Off St Helena in 1848, the creature sketched here was seen moving through the water alongside. It was sixty feet long

295 *below*
WITCH OF THE WAVE, a 1,500 ton clipper launched in 1851 for the Canton-London tea trade. She was designed by Raynes of Boston

296 *left*
The DUKE OF WELLINGTON, flagship of
the British fleet in the Baltic at the beginning
of the Crimean War. She had auxiliary screw
as well as sails. One of the last battleships
under sail, she finished as a training ship

297 *below*
British sailors at the handspikes weighing
anchor, about 1860

The Sailing Navies

Britain emerged from the Napoleonic wars with the largest fleet and the
biggest export trade of any nation in the world, and her navy maintained
upon the seven seas a degree of security hitherto unknown. The first half
of the century saw great improvements made in the sailing warships. A
rounded, apple-cheeked bow replaced the old beakhead; elliptical sterns
replaced the old square sterns with their quarter galleries; water-lines were
improved to give more speed, and a first-rate ship of the line, her old-fash-
ioned waist now enclosed to give her a flush upper deck, carried up to 130
guns. The last days of sail, however, were in sight, and the navies of the
world changed under the stress of the Crimean War and the American Civil
War from wood to iron, and canvas to coal, in less than a decade. The last
sailing battleship was the *Sanspareil* of 1851, and the first to be designed
as a steamship was the *Agamemnon* of 1852.

298 *above*
Reefing the topsails on board a merchantman
in a gale. Drawing by Huggins about 1850

299 *below*
A French brig picking up a pilot in a rough
sea. After Isabey, 1850

300 *above*
French sailors in irons, about 1820

301
An American midshipman in uniform about
1840 leaning on a capstan, with a sailor tend-
ing the touch-hole of a gun behind him

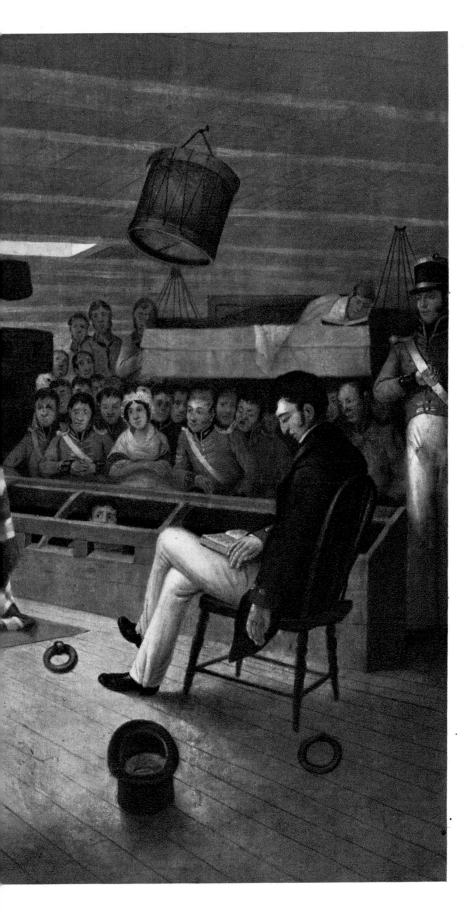

302

A church-service at sea, aboard a British man-
of-war about 1830. The Captain reads the
service, with marines on his right and midshipmen on his left. A marine officer sits
facing the Captain, and in the background a
sick man lies in his cot. The boy may be the
Captain's servant and the woman a nurse

303 *below*
A French lieutenant in his cabin, about 1840

Germany's Sailing Ships

304 *above*
The five-masted POTOSI (4,026 tons) of the
F. L. Laeisz Company, which was lost in 1927
after many memorable voyages under her
famous commander Captain Hilgendorff. She
was one of the only two five-masted clippers
ever built. The other was the PREUSSEN,
which was lost in a collision with a Channel
ferry off Dover

305 *right*
Typical seamen from a German sailing ship
in the mid-nineteenth century. Left to right:
a cook, a bo'sun and a deckhand

306 *left*
The German schooner JEA, constructed at Hamburg in about 1858

307 *below*
The port of Hamburg in the middle of the last century. This contemporary photograph well illustrates the transition from sail to steam, for although nearly all the ships in the picture are sailing ships, the notice-board advertises steamer trips

308 *left*
The first dry dock in the United States was at Gosport, Norfolk, Virginia. The DELAWARE (74 guns) in for a refit after the dock was opened in 1833

309 *below*
A famous incident in American naval history: Midshipman Spencer was hanged from the yard-arm of the United States brig SOMERS, because he 'muttered mutinously and had an odd glint in his eye'. Captain Mackenzie was tried for his murder in 1842, but acquitted

Calm Ships and Desperate Men

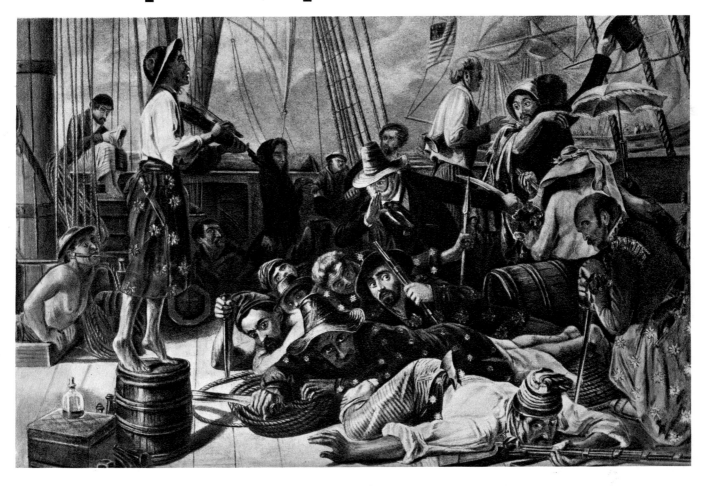

310 *above*
Pirates, disguised as peace-loving passengers, about to attack an American ship in the Caribbean in 1830. Painting by F.A. Biard

311 *left*
Keel-hauling a thief in the French navy, about 1820. The roundshot lashed to his boots kept the victim clear of a bottom foul with barnacles, on which he might otherwise have stuck like cheese on a grater. This form of punishment had been abandoned in the British navy some fifty years earlier

Smugglers and Slavers

Before the era of free trade, smuggling accounted for a large proportion of the imports to maritime nations; likewise, more slaves were exported from the west coast of Africa after the legal abolition of slavery in 1807 than before. In the 1840's some 160,000 Negroes were illegally shipped every year on the dreaded 'middle passage' to places like Cuba and Brazil, and the trade was not stifled until towards the end of the century. Piracy was stamped out by the naval patrols of nations that possessed a merchant marine, and in time the same navies put an end to the slave trade. But smuggling was never really suppressed as long as there were trade barriers between nations, and it is very likely that it will continue to flourish (as it does today in many parts of the world) as long as people wish to buy things that governments say they cannot have.

312 *below*
Offshore a slaver waits for her cargo of Negroes from West Africa, who are being taken out in native boats through the surf. On the left are the barracoons, where the slaves were kept till a ship called for them. About 1830

313 *opposite*
A diagram of the 'cargo' stowed on board the slaver VIGILANTE, captured in the Bight of Benin, 1822. She was a vessel of 240 tons, and she carried 345 slaves manacled below decks. They were packed so tight that some lay, while others sat, throughout the long 'middle passage' across the Atlantic

The representation of the brig Vigilante from Nantes, a vessel employed in the Slave Trade, which was captured by Lieutenant Mildmay, in the River Bonny, on the Coast of Africa, on the 15th of April 1822. She was 240 Tons burden & had on board, at the time she was taken 345 Slaves. The Slaves were found lying on their backs on the lower deck, as represented below, those in the centre were sitting, some in the posture in which they are there shewn & others with their legs bent under them, resting upon the soles of their feet.

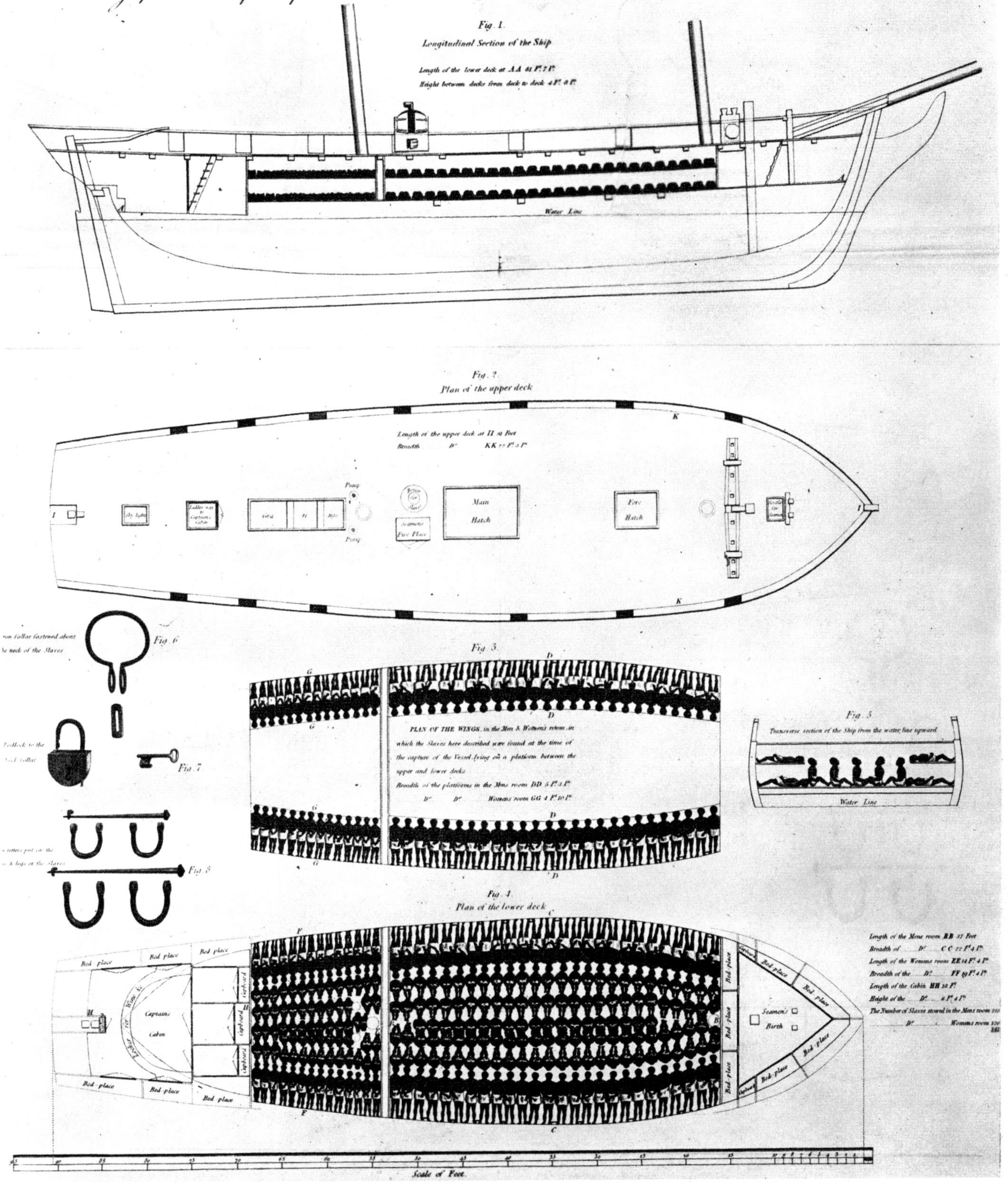

Fig. 1.
Longitudinal Section of the Ship

Length of the lower deck at AA 81 F. 3 I.
Height between decks from deck to deck 4 F. 8 I.

Fig. 2.
Plan of the upper deck

Length of the upper deck at II 81 Feet
Breadth Do KK 22 F. 2 I.

Water Line

Fig. 6.
Iron collar fastened about the neck of the Slaves

Fig. 7.

Fig. 8.

PLAN OF THE WINGS, in the Men & Womens room, in which the Slaves here described were found at the time of the capture of the Vessel, lying on a platform, between the upper and lower decks.

Breadth of the platforms in the Mens room DD 5 F. 4 I.
Do Do Womans room GG 4 F. 10 I.

Fig. 5.
Transverse section of the Ship from the water line upward

Water Line

Fig. 4.
Plan of the lower deck

Bed place

Captains Cabin

Seamen's Birth

Length of the Mens room BB 47 Feet
Breadth of Do CC 22 F. 4 I.
Length of the Womans room EE 14 F. 4 I.
Breadth of the Do FF 19 F. 4 I.
Length of the Cabin HH 10 F.
Height of the Do 6 F. 4 I.
The Number of Slaves stowed in the Mens room
Do Womans room

Scale of Feet.

175

314 *above*
HMS ACORN of the West African squadron (1841) in pursuit of the slaver GABRIEL. Slavery was legally abolished in 1807, but reached its peak in the 1840's, when the trade was mainly in the hands of Portuguese

315 *above, right*
Slaves aboard HMS DAPHNE, on their way to Mauritius after being liberated from Arab slaving dhows in the Indian Ocean. Slaves liberated in Atlantic waters were taken to Sierra Leone

316 *right*
A mixed cargo of highly dutiable goods, at a period of English history (1820) when smugglers carried 25 per cent of the nation's imports

317 *left*
The smuggler's cove, the smuggler's ship and the smuggler's cave, illumined by the artistic necessity of a blazing fire, which no sane smuggler would have lit in such circumstances. The merchandise is probably brandy

318 *below*
The loss of the packet ROYAL CHARLES off Anglesey in 1859. She was carrying passengers from Holyhead to Dublin

Slaves, Smugglers and Tempest

319 *above*
Lloyd's of London, the international insurance market and world centre of shipping intelligence. This print by Rowlandson shows the Subscription Room in the old Royal Exchange where Lloyd's was established in 1774

320 *below, left*
The Lutine Bell, salvaged from the wreck of HMS LUTINE, lost off the Dutch coast in 1799. It still hangs in Lloyd's, where one stroke of the bell heralds bad news, and two strokes good news

321 *below*
The new Underwriting Room at Lloyd's, where underwriters sit at 'boxes', reminiscent of the coffee-house booths where Lloyd's had its origins. Here is transacted business brought by Lloyd's brokers from all over the world

Laws of the Sea

As the world grew smaller and more crowded, and the oceans carried more traffic to ports ever less remote, the ancient sea-laws of Rhodes, Venice and Amalfi found a new expression in the much needed merchant shipping Acts of the nineteenth century. These Acts gave legal rights to sailors and reduced the appalling overcrowding of emigrant vessels, and the overloading of cargo ships.

322 *left*, 323 *above*
The Plimsoll Line on a modern ship. L R stands for Lloyd's Register. Other letters denote summer and winter loading-lines in various latitudes. Samuel Plimsoll (above) led the attack on overloaded 'coffin-ships' which resulted in the Merchant Shipping Act of 1871, that first ensured the right of a seaman to sail in a safe ship

324 *below*
The breeches-buoy, by which men can be taken off a wreck or lighthouse, was invented by Captain Manby in 1812

Discovery
of the
Poles

325 *above*
Parry's HECLA in Baffin Bay, 1819. She was the first ship to carry canned provisions on a voyage of exploration

326 *left*
The loss of Franklin and all his men on their quest in 1848 for the North-West Passage led to a prolonged search for survivors. This group, planning the search in London, includes Parry (fourth from left, standing) and Beaufort, inventor of the Beaufort scale of wind-force (sitting, left). Franklin's portrait hangs on the wall, left

327 *below*
Shackleton's ENDURANCE in pack-ice in 1916. He attempted to cross the Antarctic, but his ship was crushed in ice in the Weddell Sea, and the party escaped by a hazardous boat journey to South Georgia

328 *opposite*
Captain Scott's TERRA NOVA in the Ross Sea in 1911, photographed by H. G. Ponting. Though beaten to the Pole by Amundsen, Scott's journey was the most heroic on record. He died on the return trip

The Last Days of Sail

Speed and punctuality are fundamental necessities to industrial man; threaten either, and he falls into a frenzy of insurance or invention. Both are essential to the notion of progress. The steam engine provided both, on land and sea, and its development during the course of a few decades seemed so remarkable to contemporaries that apprehension was mixed with their delight. The freedom from wind and tide that the marine steam-engine gave, meant the inevitable death of the sailing ship.

The wind still blew, however, and it was some time before the early fires down below, which, because of inefficient boilers, consumed vast quantities of fuel, outmatched the breezes up aloft. The transition was not completed for almost a hundred years. During this period sailing ships were built bigger,

329 *below*
The clipper TORRENS, 1,335 tons, made the London-Adelaide run in sixty-eight days. The last of the passenger clippers, she was 222 feet in length and 38 feet beam. In 1893 Joseph Conrad served aboard her as mate, and she was broken up in 1910

faster and more beautiful than they had ever been. Merchantmen and men-of-war, survey ships and fishing boats, whalers and coasters, sealers and smugglers, penetrated every corner of the seven seas before their day was done. In some of its many ultimate forms, the sailing ship came very near to perfection: that is the real consolation to those who mourn its passing. Even when the boiler fires had triumphed and the hardy race of seamen bred to the sail had left the sea and become technicians of engines, sailing ships were still built and used on the long runs where time did not matter quite so much. They kept the tradition alive until the mid-twentieth century. But now these too have gone, and today sailing ships survive in the West only as training ships for boys and pleasure boats for sport and cruising. The immense growth of the popularity of small-boat sailing in recent years preserves much of the spirit of those who tussled with the wind long ago.

330 *above*
The set of the sails

331 *below*
The barque PARMA, of which Commander Alan Villiers was part owner, sailing under the Finnish flag in 1935

332 *above*
Cadets furling sail on the yard of the EAGLE,
a US Coast Guard vessel

333 *above*
Manning the capstan of the GRACE HARWOR in the 1930's

334 *below*
The US Coast Guard training ship EAGLE

335
'Aloft and furl.' On board a
Cape Horner in the 1930's

CHAPTER XI
The Triumph of Steam

In the month of June 1818 a three-masted vessel, apparently on fire, was seen approaching the Irish coast from westward. By the time she reached Cork her fires were no longer burning because she had run out of coal, though she had used her engines for only eighty-five hours during her twenty-seven days passage from Georgia to Liverpool. After continuing to Leningrad (then called St Petersburg) her captain, Moses Rogers, took her back to the United States, but she was wrecked on Long Island before she reached port. The voyage of the *Savannah* was the culmination of many experiments in adapting the steam engine to the ship in America, Britain and France, where river and coastal steamers had been in operation for the past ten years. Now the passenger run across the Atlantic became the proving ground of new steamships because the financial rewards were higher if a regular and punctual service could be maintained. In course of time the mail steamer became the passenger liner, sailing at scheduled times independent of wind and weather. After Samuel Cunard had founded his famous line, the Blue Ribbon of the Atlantic crossing became the prize at which all great passenger liners aimed.

It was Isambard Kingdom Brunel, not only the greatest locomotive engineer but also the most adventurous naval architect of the century, who made steamship travel popular. With his wooden paddle-steamer *Great Western* he inaugurated the first regular service to New York. The paddles of his next ship, the *Great Britain*, were replaced at the last moment by screw

336
Robert Fulton (1765-1815), the American who built the first submersible vessel for the French and constructed torpedoes for the English before retiring to America to build steamships

337 *below*
The earliest steamship of which there is any pictorial record, the American steamer PER-SEVERANCE, built by John Fitch at Philadelphia in 1786. She had a rack of paddles operated by a steam engine

338 *right*

The CLERMONT, the first commercially successful steam vessel in the world. She was built by Robert Fulton in 1807 for service on the Hudson river between New York and Albany, but she never went to sea

339 *below*

The DEMOLOGOS, also known as FULTON THE FIRST, was the first attempt to harness steam to the uses of war. She had two hulls joined like a catamaran by a central paddle-wheel, her guns being mounted broadside. Launched in 1814 at New York, she was just too late to take part in the War of 1812

propulsion in 1843, because he at once appreciated the importance of the invention of Pettit Smith in Britain and John Ericsson in the United States. He built her hull of iron, and since this proved so stout a material, the age of the iron ship arrived. The consequence was that Britain, the leading industrial nation, maintained her supremacy in naval and merchant ships for nearly a hundred years. Brunel's last great ship, the *Great Eastern*, the largest ship to be built before the *Mauretania* fifty years later, was not a commercial success, but she was the wonder of her age because she incorporated all the new developments — paddle and screw, as well as sail, gas, electricity and all modern conveniences.

The early steamship was seldom an economic proposition because of her enormous consumption of coal, so that the bulk of the world's trade still travelled by sail until the building of the Suez Canal and the boiler improvements of the 1870's. Nor was she at all suitable for a warship.

As long as guns of small calibre were mounted broadside, the paddle-wheels made her a feeble and vulnerable ship. For this reason it was not until the coming of the screw propeller and the effectiveness of the new explosive shell was demonstrated during the Crimean War that the navies of the world

340 *below*
The first British steam vessel was the CHARLOTTE DUNDAS, built by William Symington, the father of marine engineering, in 1801. She operated only on a Scottish lake. This contemporary model shows her stern paddle-wheel between twin rudders. The paddle box lies to the side

turned to the iron-hulled, screw-propelled warship. Ericsson's monitors, with their few but enormously heavy guns, showed in the American Civil War that the days of the old ' wooden wall ' were over and those of the turret ship with big long-range guns had arrived.

The British navy was still by far the largest in the world, and it was in the French and British navies that the modern battleship evolved from a series of extraordinary sea-monsters during the last part of the century. Sail disappeared forever, and at the turn of the century the introduction of the turbine engine and the substitution of oil fuel for coal saw the climax of the development of the steamship, both for warlike and peaceful purposes. Looking back on the century which saw the triumph of the steamship, we can appreciate its importance in the creation of the modern world.

341 *above*
John Bell's COMET of 1812, the first public passenger steamer in Europe. She was used on the Clyde, the home of many future steamships. The funnel was also used as a mast. She was 28 tons, and was propelled by a four horse-power engine

342 *below*
The French packet boat PERICLES, operated by the Messageries Maritime in the 1820's. Her sail power was probably greater than her steam power

Steam bridges the Atlantic

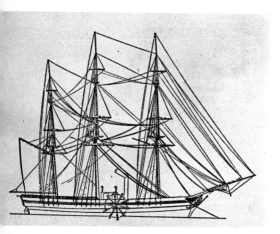

343 *left*
The American vessel SAVANNAH was the first steamer to cross the Atlantic from Georgia to Liverpool in 1818. The crossing took twenty-seven days, but she only used her engines and collapsible paddle-wheels for eighty-five hours

344 *right*
Moses Rogers (1779-1821), captain of the SAVANNAH and the first officer to take a steamship across the Atlantic and back

345 *below*
The 440-ton CURAÇAO was built at Dover, England, but sailed as a Dutch warship from Rotterdam to Curaçao in 1827, the second steamer to cross the Atlantic

346 *left*

Samuel Cunard, who was born at Halifax, Nova Scotia, in 1787, moved to Boston and thence to England. In 1839 he established the British and North American Royal Mail Steam Packet Co., which later became the Cunard Steamship Co. He died in England in 1865

347 *right*

A gentleman's cabin on board the BRITANNIA (see below), shown on a plate

348 *below*

The first Cunarder to carry mail was the BRITANNIA of 1840, a wooden paddle-steamer of 2,050 tons. Here she is seen off Boston in 1844. The winter was exceptionally severe and the citizens cut a seven-mile canal through the ice to allow her to reach the open sea. Charles Dickens sailed on her second voyage and was extremely seasick

Development of the Liner

349 *above*
The United States mail steamship PACIFIC rescuing the crew of a sinking vessel in 1852. She was one of the four American Collins-line ships which had the first bathrooms on board and took ten days to cross the Atlantic, compared to twelve taken by the Cunarders

350 *left*
The British Cunarder PERSIA which regained the Blue Ribbon in 1856. She was the largest ship in the world at that date, being three times the size of the BRITANNIA. Though screw-propelled, she retained paddle-wheels because the public distrusted screw propulsion

351 *opposite*
A Chinese impression of the first paddle-steamer to reach Canton. The nationality and date of the ship are uncertain. Similar Japanese prints commemorate the landing of Commodore Perry at Tokyo in 1853

Screw versus Paddle

352 *above*
The screw propeller which revolutionised the build of ships was invented by John Ericsson in America and Pettit Smith in Britain at about the same time. Smith named his first vessel of 237 tons the ARCHIMEDES in 1838 because her ' screwnail ' was made on the lines of an Archimedean screw rather than the propellers which replaced it

353 *left*
A scene on board the Holyhead-to-Dublin packet in 1825

354 *above*
In order to test the rival merits of screw and paddle, the British Admiralty in 1845 staged a tug-of-war between HMS RATTLER, screw-built by Brunel (left), and HMS paddle-steamer ALECTO (right). The RATTLER towed her rival through the North Sea at a rate of two mph. Each ship was about 800 tons, and the contest took place in a flat calm

355 *right*
HMS AGAMEMNON laying the Atlantic cable, which is shown fouled by a whale, in 1852. She was the first warship specifically designed to be powered by engines, but she still relied on sail for the open sea and her guns were still mounted broadside

Brunel and his Ships

356 *right*

Isambard Kingdom Brunel (1806-59), was the greatest engineer of his age. He began by building bridges in England and became chief engineer of the Great Western Railway from London to Bristol. He then turned to building the three ships shown on these two pages, which mark the transition from wood and paddle to iron and screw

357 *below*

When someone complained of the length of the Great Western Railway, Brunel replied, 'Why not make it longer and have a steamboat go from Bristol to New York?' This he did in 1838, when the GREAT WESTERN beat the time taken by her rival the SIRIUS, crossing the Atlantic in fifteen days. Her dimensions were 1,320 tons, 276 feet long, 35 feet broad

358 *above*

The GREAT BRITAIN was built by Brunel at Bristol. She was the first transatlantic liner to be built of iron and propelled by screw, though originally designed for paddles. Launched in 1843, she was later wrecked on the Irish coast, but her hull remained sound and the age of the iron ship had dawned. She is still used as a coal hulk in the Falkland Islands

359 *below*

As the GREAT EASTERN of 1858 was too large to be launched in the usual way, she was launched sideways in the Thames. She was 19,000 tons gross, 680 feet long, 82 feet broad. She was iron-built and screw-propelled, and incorporated all the new improvements such as gas. The cost of building her ruined Brunel, who died before her maiden voyage

Atlantic
Greyhounds

360 *right*
A family cabin on board the GREAT EAST-
ERN — the Victorian interior afloat

361 *far right*
The Grand Saloon (with organ) on board the
GREAT EASTERN. Though the most luxu-
rious liner of the century, she was never a
success as a passenger boat and was later
converted to lay the Atlantic and Indian ocean
cables

362 *right*
The CITY OF NEW YORK, built on the
Clyde for the American Inman Line in 1888.
Her sister ship was called the CITY OF CHI-
CAGO. These were the first twin-screw Atlan-
tic greyhounds of 10,500 tons, but they still
often used sail

War at Sea

363 *right*

A British sailor in the Crimean War (1854-6), when sailors were first given a uniform: a blouse with collar, black kerchief, bell-bottomed trousers and a broad straw hat with the ship's ribbon round it

364 *below*

HMS BULLDOG bombarding a fort in the Crimean War. The sailors wear uniform, but the Commander-in-chief, Sir Charles Napier, seen with a telescope under his arm, seems to have forgotten his cocked hat. His flag captain is properly dressed. Other officers wear caps

365 *left*
David Glasgow Farragut, the first American admiral, served as a midshipman in the War of 1812 and as commander of the Western Gulf blockading squadron in the Union forces in the Civil War

366 *below*
In 1864 Farragut's ships forced the approach to Mobile near New Orleans through a minefield and past the heavily armoured Confederate TENNESSEE (right foreground), a 'casemated' ship which engaged thirteen Union ships before her rudder was shot away. As he made the passage, he remarked, referring to the mines, 'Damn the torpedoes! Full speed ahead!'

367 *above*

The Royal Navy, by far the largest in the world in the nineteenth century, was passing through a revolution in ship-building. HMS DEVASTATION, shown in this picture, launched in 1873, may be called the first modern battleship. She incorporated all the novelties — screw, turret, iron hull, etc — and had only a short signal mast

368 *left*

The revolution in gunnery was responsible for the revolution in ship-design. This picture shows the last of the heavy muzzle-loading guns still mounted broadside in HMS ALEX-ANDRA in 1877

The Suez Canal

369 *right*
Caricature of Ferdinand de Lesseps, the French builder of the Suez Canal, forcing the continents apart. He was also responsible for the first attempt to build the Panama Canal, which failed for financial reasons

370 *below*
A contemporary view of the opening of the Suez Canal in 1869, showing the first ships passing through. The canal spelled the death of sailing ships, which could not use the Red Sea because of its unpredictable winds. The route to the East was now immeasurably shortened, and the P. and O. Company replaced the old East India Company

Men of War

371 *below*
A rare photograph of the deck of the first MONITOR, which defeated the VIRGINIA (ex-MERRIMACK) in 1862 in Hampton Roads. Designed by John Ericsson (1803-89) for the Union forces, this screw-propelled ship, mounting two 9-inch guns in one turret (in background), revolutionised the design of warships, but since she was of such shallow draft, she sank in the open sea. She was called 'a cheese box on a raft' because of the single round turret on deck

372 *above*
Launching a monitor at Brooklyn in 1862.
These later monitors — so called because they
were merely floating batteries — had two turrets, one on either side of the funnel amidships

373 *below*
The British equivalent of the monitor was
the CAPTAIN built by Captain Coles in 1870.
She sank with all hands in a storm in the
Bay of Biscay because the Admiralty insisted
on her carrying full sail rig

374
The SARDEGNA, one of the earliest Italian
battleships, was built in 1890. Her principal
armament consisted in four guns in two turrets, and her speed was 18 knots

CHAPTER XII
Sea-power in the Twentieth Century

The present century has seen the rise of three sea-powers, German, Japanese and American. The first major war in which the United States Navy was engaged was that against Spain in 1898. The Japanese navy leapt into prominence with its victory over the Russian fleet at Tsushima in 1905, one of the most complete victories in history. And by 1914 Germany had built the second most powerful navy in the world. Britain, though she emerged victorious from two world wars, endured such an economic strain in her fight for survival that her previous position as mistress of the seas suffered a relative decline. Before the First World War, over 45 per cent of the world's shipping sailed under the British flag. At the end of the Second War it had been reduced to 18 per cent, and the navy of the United States was four times the size of all other navies combined.

The German attempt to rival Britain in naval power was a principal reason for the latter's participation in the First World War. The ship-builders of Hamburg, Bremen and Kiel showed themselves masters of their craft. They built almost unsinkable warships and some of the finest liners in modern times. It was only in maritime strategy that Germany failed.

In 1906 the battleship attained the climax of its development in the 'all-big-gun' *Dreadnought*, while the submarine was regarded as little more than a dangerous toy. But after the battle of Jutland and the submarine war on

375 *below*
HMS DREADNOUGHT, the 'all big-gun' battleship, designed by Admiral Fisher in 1906. Her 12-inch guns in five turrets and her exceptional speed of 21 knots made all other big ships obsolete. In the arms race that preceded the First World War the Germans replied to the DREADNOUGHT with the KOENIG class, which in turn was superseded by the QUEEN ELIZABETH class with 15-inch guns

376 *left*
Design for a submarine in 1804. In addition to his steamships, the American Robert Fulton invented a vessel called the NAUTILUS, which submerged in the Seine near Paris in 1801. He was then invited to England where he designed this vessel, but she was so secret that no details have survived. The top half of the picture shows her under sail on the surface; the bottom half shows her submerged

377 *above*
Submarine craft could not be fully developed until the advent of electricity. This French boat, the GOUBET of 1888, was the first to use batteries. Self-propelled torpedoes were mounted on either side of the hull

trade, which was one of the reasons that brought the United States into the war in 1917, it was the submarine with her torpedoes — and afterwards the aircraft with its bombs — that spelled the death of the heavily-gunned ship. Although thirteen million tons of shipping were lost in that war, world tonnage was greater after it than before, owing to the emergence of two new ship-building powers, Japan and the United States. Since the European nations had been bled white by the war, a new order of sea-power was established at the Washington Conference of 1922, when the realities of the new situation were mirrored in the capital ship ratio permitted to the three principal navies, British, American and Japanese, in the proportions of 2:2:1. As naval aviation was not affected by this agreement, the aircraft carrier was developed at the expense of the battleship. Such ships proved of decisive importance in World War II, particularly in the Pacific, where in 1942 the battles of Midway and the Coral Sea opened a new epoch in naval warfare, for each side hardly ever saw the ships of its opponent except from aircraft flown off carriers.

The other principal weapon developed in the present century has been the submarine. In 1917, and again in 1940-43, the battle of the Atlantic was the background to all other operations. Efficient convoy organisation and radar defeated the U-boats, but the work of the American submarines was one of

378 *below*
The first modern submarine, the HOLLAND, was designed by John Philip Holland (1842-1914), an Irish-born American inventor. Launched at Elizabethport, New Jersey, in 1897, she was powered by a 45 horse-power gasoline engine for surface cruising, and a dynamotor for running submerged. Her maximum range was about 1,000 miles on the surface, and 60 miles submerged. A schematic drawing by a contemporary artist

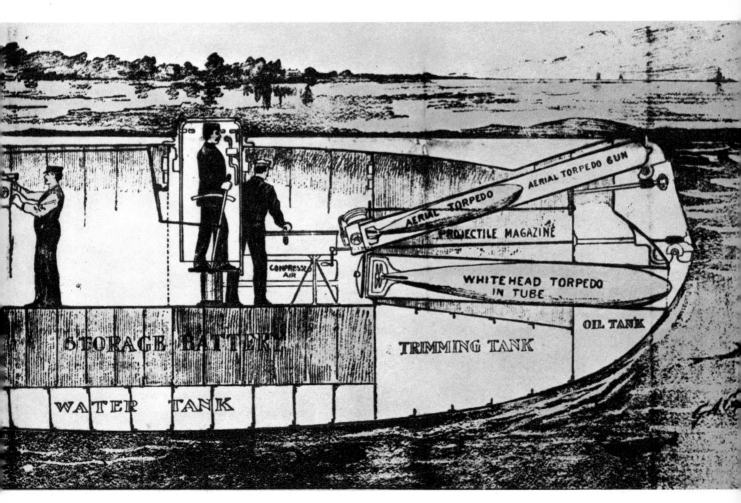

the chief causes of the Japanese defeat in the Pacific. With the invention of the nuclear submarine, and the Polaris missile fired from it while submerged, it would appear that the future of naval power lies under or over the sea, rather than on it. The new Soviet navy may not have developed the aircraft carrier, but its force of nearly five hundred submarines is a very powerful threat to the West.

Merchant shipping during the last fifty years has seen an increase in specialisation — ice-breakers, whaling factories, cableships, refrigerating ships, and, above all, tankers. Of the three main categories of modern shipping — liners, tramps and tankers — the first was so uneconomic to run that many governments subsidised their big ships for prestige reasons in order to win the Blue Ribbon. Only after the Second War did the United States enter the race, partly because the two British *Queens* had proved so fine an investment in wartime as well as in peace. In tramp-shipping the smaller nations made great advances. Scandinavian, Dutch and Greek vessels were to be seen in ports once visited only by the British. But owing to the steadily increasing dependence of civilised nations on oil fuel, the tanker fleet has made the most startling development of all. Today there are some 3,000 tankers afloat, barely forty years after the first tanker was launched, and every year they grow larger.

379 *below*
The Italian torpedo-boat in which Commander Rizzio torpedoed the Austrian battleship WIEN at Pola in 1917. The boat, seen here at Venice, was 52 feet long and had a speed of 26 knots

The most dramatic success of the submarine
was the sinking of the Cunard liner LUSI-
TANIA in May 1915. The Germans celebrated
the event by striking this medal, which shows
American passengers, then neutral, purchasing
tickets from Death in the Cunard office. The
motto at the top means, 'Business above all'

381 *below*
A German U-boat in 1917, when the submarine
attack on British and allied shipping showed
the potentiality of this form of warfare

World War I

382 *above*
The Cunarder MAURETANIA, built in 1907, held the transatlantic record of 25 knots for twenty-two years. To avoid the fate of her sistership LUSITANIA, she was camouflaged in dazzling diamonds

383 *below*
The British battleship QUEEN ELIZABETH in 1915. Mounting five 15-inch guns, she was the most powerful ship afloat. She and the WARSPITE of the same class took part in both World Wars

384 *above*
The Grand Fleet, composed of British and American ships, in the Firth of Forth in 1918. A dramatic photograph taken from the airship R 9, showing a number of battleships below the Forth Bridge

385 *right*
The surrender of the German High Seas Fleet in November 1918. The QUEEN ELIZABETH in the foreground leads the line of German ships to Scapa Flow, where they were soon afterwards scuttled by their German crews in protest against the Treaty of Versailles

The Aircraft Carrier

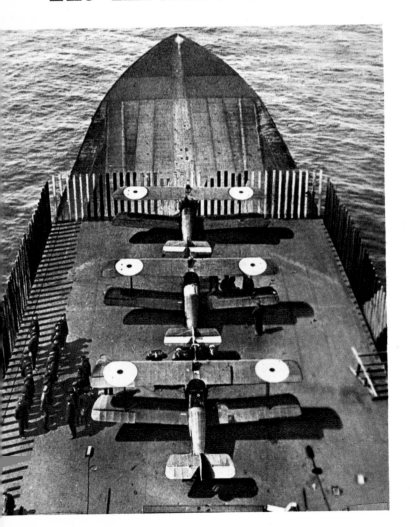

386 *above*
USS LANGLEY, the first American carrier, was converted in 1912 from the collier JUPITER by building a flight-deck over the hull. Note the horizontal smoke-ducts

387 *left*
The flight-deck of HMS FURIOUS in 1916, showing wind-shields to protect the aircraft

388 *below*
Commander Dunning landing a Sopwith Pup on the deck of the FURIOUS in 1916, one of the earliest deck-landings ever made. Immediately after this photograph was taken, the aircraft was blown overboard and her pilot killed

389 *above*
The largest carrier ever built, USS FOR-
RESTAL, launched at Newport News, Virginia, in 1954. She is 1,039 feet long, 252 feet
broad, 75,000 tons, and has a speed of 33
knots. Note the angled deck (a British invention) to facilitate landing aircraft

390 *right*
A landing signal officer guiding an American
F6F pilot on to the deck of USS ESSEX in
1945

World War II

391 *above*
The German pocket-battleship ADMIRAL GRAF SPEE, scuttled off Montevideo on 13 December 1939, after her encounter with Commodore Harwood's squadron in the battle of the River Plate

392 *below*
The 35,000 ton Italian battleship VITTORIO VENETO was one of four in her class. Built at Trieste in 1937, she carried nine 15-inch guns. She was the flagship of the squadron engaged at the battle of Matapan against Admiral Cunningham in 1941

393 *above*
A British human torpedo or 'chariot' used in the successful attack on the TIRPITZ, the largest German battleship, in a Norwegian fiord in 1942. The Italian and Japanese navies used similar craft

394 *right*
A German bomb-proof U-boat pen at Trondheim, Norway

395 *above*
Pearl Harbor, 7 December 1941. Seven out
of nine American battleships were sunk in
'Battleship Row'. A Japanese air-photo-
graph taken during the attack

396 *right*
The 15-inch guns of a battleship of the KING
GEORGE V class on convoy duty in Arctic
waters in 1943. The convoys to Russia were
the most arduous of all naval assignments

From Disaster to Victory

397 *right*
HMS ARK ROYAL was torpedoed in the Mediterranean in November 1941 with the loss of only one man. Commissioned in 1938, she had steamed 200,000 miles without a refit. A carrier of 27,000 tons, she had a flight-deck 800 feet long

398 *below*
United States landing-craft approaching a beach during manoeuvres in 1945. Each of these assault vessels carried thirty-five men, and they decided the war in the Pacific

Ships of Today

399 *above*
The prototype of some of the largest vessels
afloat today. The VULCANUS of 1910, the first
of the tankers. She was 1,180 tons and was
built at Amsterdam

400 *below*
The EUGENIA NIARCHOS, built by Vickers-
Armstrong in 1956 for the Greek ship-owner
and sailing under the Liberian flag. She is
the largest tanker yet constructed — 47,000
tons and carrying sixteen million gallons of
oil — but 80,000-ton tankers are under construction in Japan for the Niarchos and
Onassis lines

401 *above*
The Cunarder QUEEN MARY arriving at
New York on her maiden voyage in 1936,
having achieved a record mean speed of 30.63
knots. She is 1,019 feet long, 81,235 tons,
and can carry 2,340 passengers

402 *below*
The new flagship of the Italia Line, the LEO-
NARDO DA VINCI, was launched at Genoa
in December 1958 and made her maiden voyage
across the Atlantic in July 1960. She is 33,000
tons, 761 feet long and 92 feet beam, and
has accommodation in three classes for 1,326
passengers. Her cruising speed is 23 knots

403 right
USS MISSOURI in a rough sea during the Korean war in 1951. A battleship of the Iowa class, she carries nine 16-inch guns. Launched in 1944, she is one of the last of the battleships

404 below
The first atomic submarine, NAUTILUS, of a type which is capable of circumnavigating the entire globe without surfacing. She was launched in 1954 as the first of thirty-seven nuclear submarines, several of which have already sailed under the North Pole. The future of the warship seems to lie with this type of vessel

405 *above*

A beautiful photograph by the U.S. Navy of 'Task Group Alfa' on exercises in the North Atlantic in August 1959. The task group's main purpose is to develop tactics to combat potential submarine threats to the United States. The flagship, USS VALLEY FORGE, is surrounded by destroyers and submarines, while patrol aircraft fly overhead

406 *right*

The launching of the Polaris rocket from a submerged submarine in July 1960. At the time of the test, the American submarine was cruising in the Atlantic about thirty miles off the coast of Florida. The rocket covered more than a thousand miles before returning into the sea. The range has now been extended to 1,600 miles

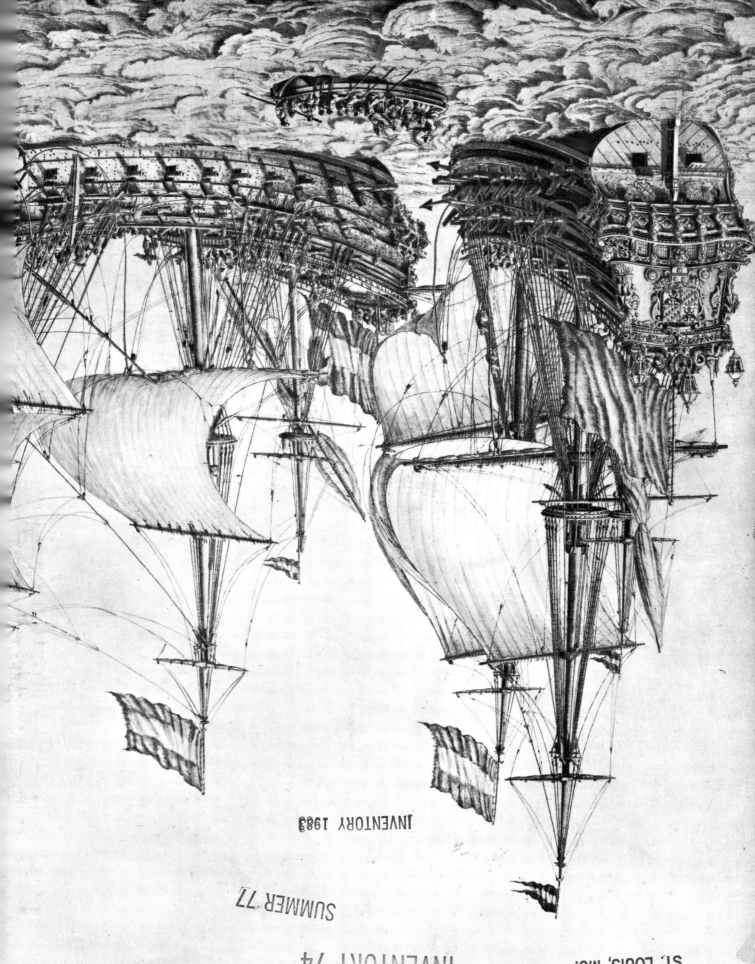